The New Testament
A STUDY

By

HERBERT C. ALLEMAN

MUHLENBERG PRESS
PHILADELPHIA : PENNSYLVANIA

COPYRIGHT, 1935, BY
THE BOARD OF PUBLICATION OF
THE UNITED LUTHERAN CHURCH IN AMERICA

MADE IN THE UNITED STATES OF AMERICA
UE302

To J. S. A.

INTRODUCTION

THE importance of leadership education in the church is universally acknowledged. The rapid development in general education, the influence exerted by these developments upon Christian education, and the production of new types of courses for church schools and church societies are making greater demands upon church workers. These cannot be fully met without at least a measure of preparation on the part of all who are responsible for carrying on the various activities of the local congregation and its auxiliary organizations. This need of more adequate leadership preparation has been felt not only by the leaders of the church at large but also by the local church workers themselves. There is evident everywhere an earnest desire for a program of leadership education which will help present and prospective congregational leaders to equip themselves for more effective service.

The United Lutheran Church in America, through its Parish and Church School Board, has for many years been aware of this need of its constituency and has planned a series of texts to help meet the requirements of the present educational situation in the church. This series of texts is known as *The Lutheran Leadership Course*.

The Board has recognized the fact that some church workers have had more educational advantages and fuller leadership experiences than others. Accordingly, it has planned courses on two levels—a more elementary series and a somewhat advanced series. The present volume is a text in the more advanced series.

This text is intended to provide the basic material for a course on the New Testament. There are numerous possible approaches to a study of the New Testament. For example, the New Testament may be studied as the culmination of the record of God's revelation; or, it may be viewed from the angle of its spiritual power in the lives of men; or, it may be treated as a book of divine truths having preaching and teaching values; or, it may be regarded primarily as a devotional book to be read by devout souls for the upbuilding of their personal faith and life; or, it may be considered historically in order that the student may see how this sacred book came into being through the instrumentality of human writers whom God used to give to the world a true record of his divine revelation in Jesus Christ, his Son. In other words, the New Testament may be studied dogmatically, or spiritually, or homiletically, or devotionally, or historically. Each of these approaches is thoroughly valid and each has its own peculiar significance and worth. In view of the fact that most church workers are familiar with the New Testament as a book of divine revelation, an inspired record, a means of grace, a spiritual guide, and a basis for personal devotions—this because of their attendance in church schools, catechetical classes, and church services—and in view of the fact that few of them have had an opportunity to study the New Testament in its historical setting, this textbook has been prepared entirely from the historical angle. Throughout this volume, therefore, it is assumed that the student has an appreciation of the New Testament as an inspired record of divine revelation and as a book of divine truth which possesses spiritual power to bring God's salvation in Jesus Christ, his Son, to the souls of men. The purpose of this text—and this limitation should be clearly noted at the outset and kept in mind throughout the study—is to set forth clearly, and as accurately as present knowledge allows, the historical development of the writings of the New Testament together with a brief sketch of the content of each book.

While this text is limited by its purpose, instructors should feel free to add interpretations and to make applications of the content materials here presented. The class sessions should be something more than lecture periods in which the content of these chapters is merely restated, and something more than mere question-and-answer periods in which students are asked merely to review the material in the text. Instructors' methods will naturally vary, but student participation in research and in class discussions is highly desirable. This course may be offered as a one-unit course or as a two-unit course. When given as a one-unit course, it is expected that from ten to twelve class periods will be devoted to it. In this case the material found in the body of the text should be given primary consideration. When given as a two-unit course, two hours of class work should be devoted to each chapter, instead of one hour as in the case of a one-unit course. When the course is taken for two credits, much use should be made of the suggestions found in the supplements to the various chapters. (See the note at the beginning of the "Supplement to Chapter I.") For credit requirements, *The Lutheran Leadership Course Bulletin* should be consulted.

Students taking this course on the New Testament should not only study the text itself, but should do as much Bible reading as possible. The references under "Bible Readings" at the beginning of each chapter should be considered a minimum requirement. The "Bibliography" is intended primarily for instructors, though the books listed will prove helpful also to students who desire to investigate more thoroughly the subject under consideration. The "Questions" found at the end of the narrative are placed there largely to help the student focus his attention upon the main points in the chapter; they will serve, therefore, as a means for review.

The author of the present text, the Rev. Herbert C. Alleman, D.D., has been chosen to prepare it because of his specialized knowledge in the field of the Bible and because of his more than twenty years of experience in teaching. He is a professor in the Lutheran Theological Seminary at Gettysburg, Pa., and has also taught extensively in leadership training groups. This volume is highly recommended to all church workers who desire a better understanding of the background and content of the New Testament.

Due acknowledgment is hereby made to the International Council of Religious Education for their kind permission to quote from the American Standard Edition of the Revised Bible, copyright, 1929.

CONTENTS

		PAGE
I.	The Background of the New Testament	11
II.	The Origin of the New Testament	26
III.	The Gospels according to Matthew and Luke	38
IV.	The Gospel according to John	50
V.	The Life and Teaching of Jesus	62
VI.	The Church in Palestine	77
VII.	The Extension of the Church to the Gentiles	86
VIII.	The Gospel in Europe	99
IX.	The Epistle to the Romans	113
X.	Captivity Epistles and Pastoral Epistles	121
XI.	The Other Epistles and Revelation	132
XII.	New Testament Institutions	143

CHAPTER I

THE BACKGROUND OF THE NEW TESTAMENT

The New Testament Scriptures are the record of a great fact and its meaning for the world. The fact is the life and ministry of Jesus. It is the most significant fact in history. The person, life, and work of Jesus were the creative source of a new movement in human history which opened the door of hope to a despairing world. The New Testament Scriptures grew out of that great fact; the Gospel came before the New Testament was written. The men who wrote it at first did not realize what they had experienced. They came to write the New Testament books only when this realization was borne in upon them by the Spirit of God in the growing life of the new fellowship of faith which we call the Christian Church. The New Testament Scriptures did not create the church but grew out of it and are witnesses of it. We must understand that creative fact before we can understand the books. It came at a definite time and place in history. It can be located. It has its historical background.

1. *The Land in Which the Gospel Came.* The Christian Gospel had its historical origin in Palestine. Though this country is a small land—only a shell of mountain and a rim of shore—it has had a hold on human interest such as no other country has had. Embracing only about 11,000 square miles of territory, it is a land of many varied contrasts. Its altitudes range from 10,000 feet above sea level to 1,300 feet below. Its landscape combines mountains and plains, rivers and seas, forests and fertile fields, cultivable hills and barren wastes. It is doubtful whether any other territory of equal size offers such varied prospects.

Interesting as Palestine is to the eye, it is more interesting in history. Nature made this little land a bridge between Eurasia and Africa. Over this bridge passed the armies of world conquerors from Sargon to Napoleon, and over it also passed the caravans of trade between Egypt and Mesopotamia. Palestine has been a football of empires in a great war-game which began sixteen centuries before Christ and may not be at an end even now. In a lull in the drama of history this land was taken possession of by the people of promise and became the sanctuary of their religion. And here, in the fullness of time, Christ, the world's Saviour, was born for the healing of the nations. In the narrow belt between the northern and the southern hills his ministry was performed, and in its capital he was crucified.

In Jesus' day Palestine was divided into four parts: Judea, Samaria, Galilee, and Perea. The first three of these lay to the west of the Jordan; the fourth, to the east of it.

Judea, the most southerly of the divisions to the west, corresponded roughly with the old kingdom of Judah, though now the Philistine country along the Mediterranean Sea was included in it. Jerusalem was its capital. While Jerusalem was the capital only of Judea, it was, nevertheless, the religious center of the entire land. It was the Holy City, whose Temple, with its thousand years' prestige, drew all loyal Jews to its great feasts.

Samaria, immediately to the north of Judea, included the hills of northern Benjamin and of Ephraim together with the broad, fertile valleys which stretched out between them. It was a territory more pleasing to the eye than Judea, and also richer in natural resources. It was inhabited by a mongrel people, the descendants of a stock of mixed Israelites and Babylonians.

Galilee, to the north of Samaria, included the plain of Esdraelon and the low hills and fertile valleys of Zebulun and Naphtali. In the extreme north its mountains merge with the Lebanon ranges, with mount Hermon on the east. Just to the east of Galilee is the sea bearing the same name. It lies like a harp in the embrace of the surrounding hills. Being 681 feet below sea level, it has a tropical climate. Today it is almost deserted, but in Jesus' day its coast was a populous, busy place, with nine cities, each said to have had more than 15,000 inhabitants. Along its western and northern shores lay a great caravan route, which brought trade and commerce to the region. Some of the ten cities of the Decapolis (a league of cities for commercial purposes somewhat like the Hanseatic cities of medieval Europe) were situated around the lake, and these were flourishing centers of Greek culture.

Perea, on the east of the Jordan, extended from the valley of

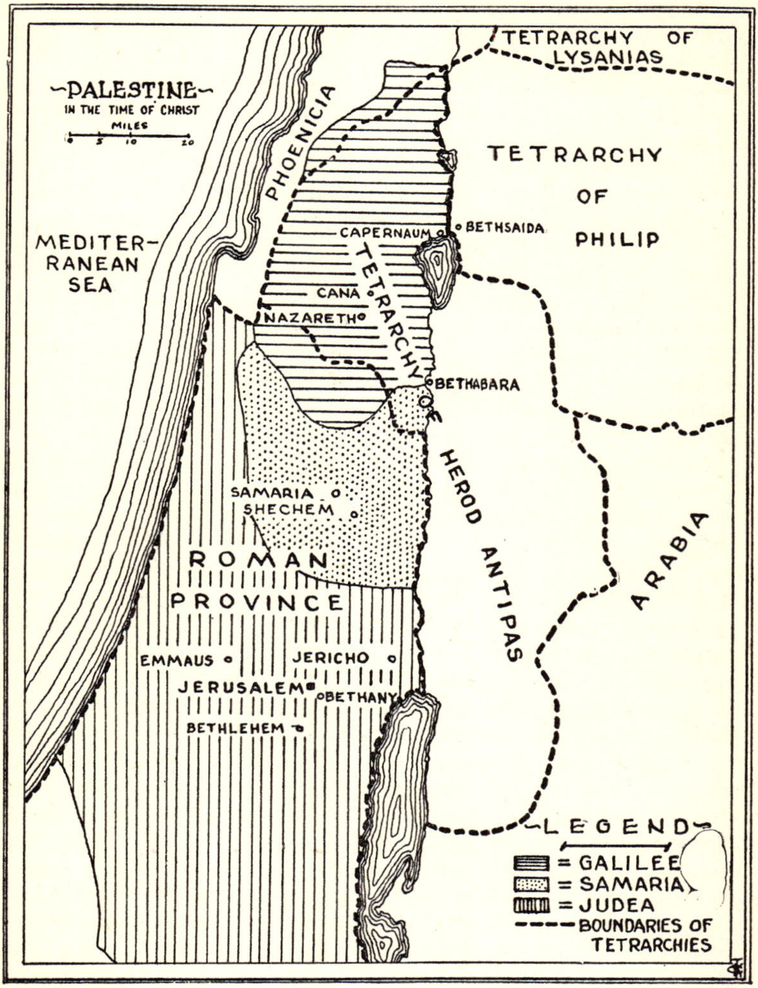
PALESTINE
IN THE TIME OF CHRIST
MILES
0 5 10 20
MEDITER-RANEAN SEA
PHOENICIA
TETRARCHY OF LYSANIAS
TETRARCHY OF PHILIP
CAPERNAUM
BETHSAIDA
TETRARCHY OF HEROD ANTIPAS
CANA
NAZARETH
BETHABARA
SAMARIA
SHECHEM
ROMAN PROVINCE
EMMAUS
JERICHO
JERUSALEM
BETHANY
BETHLEHEM
ARABIA
LEGEND
= GALILEE
= SAMARIA
= JUDEA
BOUNDARIES OF TETRARCHIES

the Yarmuk, just below the Sea of Galilee, to the valley of the Arnon, about midway along the length of the Dead Sea. It included Gilead and the northern half of Moab. Many Jews resided in this region during the time of Jesus' ministry.

2. *The Political Situation.* At the time of Jesus' birth, the ancient world-powers which had dominated the Old Testament picture were dead, and a new lord of nations had arisen to take their place. This new power was Rome, whose empire, at the time of Jesus, embraced southern Europe and a part of northern Africa, while Syria, Egypt, and Asia Minor were practically its dependencies. Rome was mistress of the civilized world. How had this come about?

The scepter of world empire had passed from Babylon to Assyria, from Assyria back to Babylon, thence to Persia, and thence to Greece. After the death of Alexander the Great, two of his generals, Ptolemy of Macedonia and Seleucus of Antioch, fought to succeed him, but in the end their successors wore each other out and opened the door for the subsequent conquest by the Romans. Palestine was the unhappy frontier between the two kingdoms, which now centered in Egypt and in Syria. The Jews themselves were not attacked until Antiochus Epiphanes, halted by the Romans from any further advance against Egypt, turned upon the land of Palestine in his fury, determined to make it the southern border of his kingdom. In his rashness Antiochus desecrated the Temple and made it a heathen sanctuary. Stung to madness by this sinister act, the Jews rallied about a patriotic leader, Mattathias, and his heroic sons. Under the leadership of one of these sons, Judas, called Maccabeus (meaning "the hammer"), the Jews succeeded in freeing their land from the hated Seleucid rule. The Maccabees then proceeded to exterminate every trace of Greek influence and to Judaize the whole land by force. It was a grim and terrible movement—a flare-back of fanatic zeal because of all that the Jews had suffered. Probably nothing else would have saved the Jews for an independent destiny.

But the short-lived political independence that the Maccabees built up, the Romans, with the help of the Herods, destroyed. The Herods were descendants of a certain Antipater, governor of Idumea (the district south of Palestine). The Maccabees were disrupted by a wily intrigue and this led to their defeat.

It was at this juncture, when the Maccabees were divided against themselves, that the Romans appeared upon the scene. They had absorbed Italy, northern Africa, Greece, and Syria, and they were now preparing to win the East. The leader of this Roman conquest was Pompey. In 64 B. C. he moved into Galilee; a year later he captured Jerusalem. Rome became the established power, and the Herods were her deputies. Herod the Great (37-4 B. C.), who "stole his throne like a fox, ruled like a tiger, and died like a dog," was the most famous of this despised line. He ruthlessly put to death all who stood in his way and sought fame in the most extravagant building program the land had ever known. He rebuilt Samaria and Jerusalem on a splendid scale and built Cæsarea, a miniature Rome, on the Mediterranean. But his crowning work was the rebuilding of the Temple at Jerusalem (14 B. C.). At his death his kingdom was divided among his three surviving sons—Archelaus, who was named ethnarch of Judea, Samaria, and Idumea; Antipas, who was made tetrarch of Galilee and Perea; and Philip, who was made tetrarch of the regions toward Damascus. Archelaus was thoroughly bad. Unable longer to endure his rule, the Jews made such a powerful complaint to Rome that the emperor banished him (A. D. 6) and placed his territory under a Roman procurator, or governor. These procurators resided at Cæsarea, except at the time of Jewish feasts, when they stayed in Jerusalem.

The fifth of these Roman procurators was Pontius Pilate (A. D. 26-36), during whose term of office Jesus was crucified. Under Roman rule, the high priests were the nominal leaders of the Jewish people, but in practice no important step was taken without the consent of the governor. Jewish judges made decisions in cases relating to property, and the Jewish supreme court, the Sanhedrin, held jurisdiction in religious matters and was permitted even to pass judgment in capital cases, but it had no power to carry out the sentence. Customs and taxes were collected by publicans, or tax-farmers. These men levied their dues by force, and thus the name "tax-gatherer" came to be almost synonymous with "robber" and "brigand." But the bitterest humiliation to the Jews was that the procurator reserved the right, as the Herods had in earlier days, to appoint and depose the high priest. Even the high-priestly robes were under the procurator's charge, being kept by the captain of the fort of Antonia and handed over for use only on the Day of Atonement and the three Great Feasts. The Jews could see in such indignities only "the footmarks of the Messiah," who most surely would come very soon to avenge them. During Pilate's regime, this expectation of a coming Messianic age became very strong. It was believed that the Messiah, the son of David, would come to overwhelm the heathen and to restore the kingdom of Israel. He would then make Jerusalem and the Temple the spiritual center for the whole earth.

3. *The Economic Situation.* In the New Testament period the Jews were no longer a strictly agricultural people, as they had been during the major part of the Old Testament era, but they were still dependent on their own tillage of the soil. Especially was this true in Galilee, where every available piece of ground was cultivated and where the harvests were exceedingly abundant. The country was rich in grain, vegetables, fruits, dates, and olives. Vineyards abounded, particularly in Judea and Samaria. Sheep and cattle were other sources of wealth. The Sea of Galilee was the center of a flourishing fishing industry, while the bitumen of the Dead Sea furnished a world-famous article of commerce.

Crafts and craftsmen of more than forty kinds are mentioned in the literature of the New Testament era—among them, tailors, shoemakers, builders, masons, carpenters, millers, bakers, tanners, merchants, dairymen, physicians, barbers, hairdressers, laundrymen, jewelers, smiths, weavers, dyers, embroiderers, carpet makers, well-diggers, fishermen, beekeepers, potters, coopers, pitch-refiners, glass-makers, armorers, copyists, painters, and engravers. Trades were passed on from father to son. Thus Jesus followed Joseph in his trade. There were entire families especially skilled in a single trade, who would not reveal their secret outside their own family. Whole cities were famous for one kind of work, as they still are today. Bethsaida was a city of fishermen; Magdala, of dyers; Sepphoris, of weavers; Beth-shean, of cotton spinners. Nazareth seems to have been a city of wood-workers, and Bethlehem, of shell-workers.

While there were many kinds of artisan in the time of Jesus, the great majority of the people were peasants. These peasants

—so frequently referred to in the gospels—lived together in villages, from which they went out to their patches, which they worked with their own hands. Most of their profits, however, went to the tax-gatherers. The lot of these peasants was always precarious, for one or two bad seasons would often reduce them to the status of hirelings or even cause them to be sold into slavery. In such cases, they were dependent on the labor-market, and if no one hired them, they became beggars or brigands. On the other hand, some of them, particularly in Galilee, grew prosperous and even became the creditors of their poorer neighbors. Further, there were "men of property," the lords of the land, who had stewards to handle their affairs. There were thus the extremes of a feudal society, with wealthy landowners at one end of the line and numerous slaves at the other.

Commerce and trade flourished. The original tradesmen of Palestine had been the Canaanites; but after the days of Alexander the Great the Jews developed rapidly as dealers, and, with the larger opportunities which followed the Maccabean conquests, their trade made rapid progress, even extending into foreign lands. Palestine's natural situation lent itself to trade and commerce. Some of the oldest and most famous highways of history passed through it: the old road from Damascus to Egypt; the coast road from Antioch to Tyre and southward; the road from Gaza to Petra and the East. Trade was helped, too, by the regular religious pilgrimages to Jerusalem at the time of the great festivals. However, trade had also its handicaps: brigands infested many parts of the country; religious restrictions frequently limited business opportunity; foreign currency had to be used, for the Jews had no right of coinage; and taxes were heavy.

Taxation was of two kinds—secular and religious. Beginning with the Greek period, the secular, or state, taxes included a poll tax, a salt tax, a marriage tax, a land tax, a cattle tax, and a fruit-tree tax. Export and import taxes were levied on merchandise and were collected by the publicans. There was also a frontier tax—a particularly obnoxious tax, levied at practically every stopping place along the country's thoroughfares.

In addition to these, there were religious taxes. The Law required that the people support both the priestly hierarchy and the Temple. "The contributions which the priests received from the people for their support before the Exile were variable and irregular. After the Exile, they were immeasurably increased."[1] The chief religious taxes were: (1) the priestly tithe (donations of flesh and skins of sacrificial animals, of grains, of fruits, of shewbread, etc.); (2) atonement money (financial payments for the redemption of first-born sons and of unclean animals); (3) the tithe (a part of all food and of all products of the ground); (4) the first-born of animals; (5) extraordinary dues (for example, dues for release from vows); and (6) the Temple-tax (a half-shekel annually from every adult Israelite for the upkeep of the Temple). Besides these, free-will offerings were expected. Further, the people were called upon to support also their local synagogues and schools, and—always a sacred charge—the poor of the land.

In addition to these ordinary taxes, Herod imposed upon the generation of Jesus' day a building program of appalling magnitude, which included not only the Temple but also royal palaces at Cæsarea, Tiberias, Cæsarea Philippi, Joppa, Gaza, and Jericho. It is evident that the total taxation in Jesus' day, civil and religious combined, must have approached intolerable proportions. It is no wonder that the tax-burdened, impoverished people were driven either to the violence of the zealots or to the Messianic hope of the pious. The mood of the people from the time of Pilate onward was increasingly rebellious. Each succeeding procurator had a harder and harder task. The age was slowly drifting toward revolution and war.

4. *The Religion of the Jews in Jesus' Day.* There is scarcely a chapter of the New Testament which can be accurately interpreted without at least some acquaintance with the Jewish religion of Jesus' time. What were the chief religious ideas and practices of the Jews?

Like their forefathers of the Old Testament period, the Jews of Jesus' day believed in one God. But a doctrine of angels and demons had developed, different from and in addition to that which is found in the Old Testament. The angels were numberless and formed the "heavenly host." Side by side with them are found demons, whose number is also very great. These

---

[1] Schuerer, *Geschichte*, Vol. 2, p. 297.

demons were believed to live in desert regions and in places which were unclean.

Man, it was held, had been created in the image of God, and his constituent elements were described as body, soul, and spirit. The body was from the earth; the spirit, from above; the soul, the resulting life which made man a person. The body was never thought of as evil; temptations always came from without. In man, it was believed, there was an impulse toward the good and another toward the evil. Between these two there was war. When, in this inner conflict, the evil prevailed over the good, the ultimate consequence was loss of the kingdom of God; when the good prevailed and held sway, then by practicing the precepts of the Law man attained satisfaction, or, as we might say, righteousness.

The Law was the most potent single influence in the religious life of the Jews in New Testament days. Primarily, "the Law" referred to the religious tenets and practices prescribed in the Pentateuch, but succeeding ages had produced a large body of oral law which was widely accepted as of equal authority with the written Law. It was adherence to the oral law that made Judaism what it was in Jesus' day.

The foremost requirement of the Law, according to the views of Judaism at this period, was the observance of the Sabbath. It was kept as a day of rest from toil, a day of festival character from which joy was by no means excluded. During the period of the Babylonian exile, Sabbath observance became the badge of Judaism and, as such, was guarded with strict prescriptions. These finally developed into Pharisaic legalism, against which Jesus vigorously protested.

Next to the observance of the Sabbath came the doing of "the works of the Law." These were the very heart of practical religion and consisted of almsgiving, prayer, and fasting. They were regarded as "works of righteousness," and it was the undue emphasis laid upon the first and the last that led to frequent protests by Jesus against self-righteousness.

The institutional side of Jewish religion centered, as of old, in the Temple, which was now the splendid new structure of marble and gold built by Herod the Great. In the service of the Temple there was a large personnel, headed by the high priest. Thousands of other priests, divided into twenty-four courses, and large numbers of Levites, who assisted the priests, completed the official hierarchy. Morning and evening sacrifices were offered daily, while on the Sabbaths and on the special festival days additional offerings were made.

While the Temple was the center of Judaism's institutional religion, another institution held an important place. This was the synagogue, a local, popular place of worship, where the people gathered to study the Law, to attend the preaching and teaching of the synagogue teachers, and to pray. Those who could not be present at a synagogue service observed the hour of prayer wherever they might be. In each synagogue, services were held every morning, afternoon, and evening. The three main parts of the service were: prayer, Scripture reading, and exposition, or preaching. Though the synagogue was primarily a place for religious assemblies, it was used also for other purposes, including civic and municipal functions.

Instruction was an important part of Jewish religious practice. The child's religious education began in the home. At the age of five or six the boy was sent to the synagogue school, where he came under the instruction of the synagogue teacher, the rabbi. Here he learned portions of the Pentateuch together with the oral law, which at this time included innumerable rules for the observance of the written Law. All this was learned by repeating it after the rabbi. Associated with the rabbis were the scribes, whose principal work was to copy the Law and the little parchments (phylacteries) which every pupil must have. The scribes were paid for their work; the rabbis earned their living by some handicraft and taught without compensation. It was esteemed a high honor to be a rabbi. Both the rabbis and the scribes belonged to a religious party called the Pharisees. There were five such parties in Jesus' day: the Pharisees, the Sadducees, the Essenes, the Zealots, and the Herodians.

The Pharisees were "Separatists" who, after the Maccabean struggle, associated themselves to observe the Law, both written and oral. They were a body of pious laymen, devoted to teaching the Law to the people. Their rise was "a laymen's movement" in the midst of a dead, priest-ridden land. They were held in high regard by the people and, by the time of Jesus, had become the most influential party in Judaism. They were fanatically devoted to the letter of the Law, often suspending a decision on the turn of a sentence. A specimen of Pharisaic exegesis, which Paul turns against their followers, may be seen in *Galatians 3: 16*. It was inevitable that Jesus should come into conflict with the Pharisees. He denounced them more than he denounced any other class of the people. He uncovered the hypocrisy of their religious zeal. He declared that the heart, and not external practices, determined the quality of a man's religion. There were, it is to be remembered, two groups of Pharisees in Jesus' day. One group, the school of Hillel, were advocates of a liberal interpretation of the Law; the other, the school of Shammai, were unyielding literalists. It is probable that Jesus' invective against the Pharisees was directed against the latter, while the friendly intercourse between him and the Pharisees referred to in other passages (*Lk. 7: 36; 11: 37; 14: 1; Jn. 3: 18; 19: 39*) pointed to relation with the Hillelites.

In opposition to the Pharisees stood the Sadducees. They were the priestly party, the traditional aristocracy of the land. Though less numerous than the Pharisees, they were influential because of their wealth and position. They were less religious than the Pharisees, but more conservative in theology, recognizing only the written Law. Unlike the Pharisees, who believed in a resurrection, the Sadducees rejected this belief.

The Essenes were a distinctly religious society. They were an offshoot of the Pharisees. They withdrew to the wilderness in the neighborhood of the Dead Sea and lived a celibate, monastic life. They had all things in common, were kind to the poor, and distributed liberally to the suffering. Though they were fairly numerous, they are not mentioned in the New Testament; but the work of John the Baptist reflects their influence.

The fourth party, to which the name Zealots or Cananæans was later given, was composed of young enthusiasts who had a deadly hatred for Rome and the Herods. They were intense nationalists and patriots who believed it to be a religious duty to rid the land of these foreigners, these Romans. To this end they did not hesitate to incite revolutions. They are referred to in *Matthew 11: 12*. They keenly cherished the Messianic idea, and it was perhaps one of their number, Simon the Zealot, who became a disciple of Jesus.

The personal followers and friends of the Herods constituted another party, known as the Herodians. They too were nationalists; their purpose, however, was not to drive out the Romans, but to unite the country once more under a native prince, Herod. The party was not large, but it was rich and influential.

As has been said, the Zealots keenly cherished the Messianic idea. But this idea was by no means confined to them. It was a very commonly accepted belief in the period just before the birth of Jesus. This belief in the coming of a Messiah (anointed one) to deliver Jehovah's people from the yoke of their oppressors and to establish the kingdom of God, existed from the days of the prophets. It was this hope, in its first glimmerings, which had led to the establishment of the monarchy in the days of Samuel. In those days the reigning king was viewed as "Jehovah's anointed."

The first to turn away from this idea was Isaiah. He believed and prophesied that Jehovah would send a wonderful King who would establish Jehovah's real kingdom on earth (*Isa. 9:2-7; 11:1-9*). This was the beginning of a forward look which was to sustain the Jews through many calamities and reverses. It even survived the Exile, and later, just before the Maccabean period, became the inspiration of a new type of literature, known as "apocalypse." These literary products were attributed by their anonymous authors to ancient worthies—to Enoch, the sons of Jacob, Moses, Isaiah, Baruch, Daniel, and Ezra.

Though these writings differed from one another in form, they all taught the same idea: the days of oppression and trial would end; Elijah would come again and announce the coming of the Messiah; the Messiah would appear and redeem Jehovah's people from all evil, overcome their foreign enslavers "by the breath of his lips," restore the kingdom to the house of Israel, and set up a rule of righteousness; the signs of his coming would consist of wars and tumults, the breaking up of domestic security, the terrible phenomena in earth, sea, and sky; divine judgment would then follow, in which the wicked would be sentenced to everlasting torment in Gehenna, while the righteous would receive the reward of eternal bliss in Paradise.

Such was, in brief, the geographical, political, economic, and religious background of the new religious movement which grew out of the person, life, and work of Jesus.

Questions

1. What can you tell about Palestine in Jesus' day? Describe the four main divisions of the land.

2. What nation then dominated the world? What were the historical events which led up to its control of Palestine?

3. What do you recall about the life of the Jewish people in Jesus' day? What were their chief modes of livelihood? their chief natural resources? their greatest financial burdens?

4. What did the Jews of Jesus' day believe about God? angels? demons? man? sin? salvation?

5. What were the practical aspects of Jewish religion at this time? What place had the following in the religious practices of the Jews?

>   (1) The Sabbath
>   (2) The Law
>   (3) The Temple
>   (4) The synagogue

6. Who were the priests? the Levites? the rabbis? the scribes? the Pharisees? the Sadducees? the Essenes? the Zealots? the Herodians?

7. What was the Messianic hope? How did it develop?

Bibliography

Note: Under this heading there appear in each chapter a few titles of books which have been used in the preparation of the chapter. Students desiring to pursue further their study of the subject under consideration will find these books of value.

Barton, G. A. *Jesus of Nazareth: a Biography,* 1926.
Fairweather, W. *The Background of the Gospels,* 1908.
Grant, F. C. *The Economic Background of the Gospels,* 1926.
Herford, R. T. *The Pharisees,* 1924.
Klausner, J. *Jesus of Nazareth,* Eng. tr. Herbert Danby, 1929.
McCown, C. C. *The Genesis of the Social Gospel,* 1929.
Matthews, S. *A History of New Testament Times in Palestine,* rev. ed. 1933.
Œsterley, W. O. E. *The Jewish Background of the Christian Liturgy,* 1925.

SUPPLEMENT TO CHAPTER I

Note: The suggestions found in these supplements to the various chapters are intended primarily for the use of students taking this course as a two-unit course; assignments from each of the two groups of assignments are a requirement for two units of credit. Assignments may be made also, at the discretion of the instructor, for students taking this course for a single credit. Students will find the use of Bible dictionaries, concordances, and commentaries helpful in their studies. Where no other references are given these should be consulted.

Group A—Studies in the Bible

The Ministry of Jesus and the Geography of Palestine
Read the following passages and then locate on a map the places mentioned in them: *Mark 1: 9; John 2: 11-13; 4: 3-5; Matthew 15: 21; 16: 13-17; Mark 10: 1* (this was through Perea). What territory did our Lord cover during his public ministry?

The Pharisees, the Sadducees, the Herodians
With the help of a concordance, look up in the gospels typical references to each of these Jewish parties. What was the attitude of each group toward Jesus? What was his attitude toward them?

Jesus and the Temple
What was Jesus' first appearance in the Temple? His second? His last? What was Jesus' attitude toward the Temple? Try to find answers to these questions in the Bible itself. Write a few paragraphs on the above topic, giving Biblical references.

Jesus and the Synagogue
Look up "Synagogue" in a concordance. Note the references to it in the four gospels. Read these passages carefully. Write a few paragraphs on this topic, giving Biblical references to prove your conclusions.

Jesus and Sabbath Observance
Study the following passages and endeavor to discover Jesus' attitude toward observance of the Sabbath: *Luke 4: 14-22; Mark 2: 23-28; Matthew 12: 9-13; Luke 13: 10-17.*

Group B—Topics for Further Study

The Roman Empire in the Days of Augustus
Make a careful study of the Roman Empire in the days of Augustus, giving especial attention to its extent, its government, its policies in its treatment of conquered peoples, its means of communication, its economic life. Encyclopedias and historical reference books will prove helpful. Consult also F. C. Grant's *The Economic Background of the Gospels*, Chap. I.

THE NEW TESTAMENT—A STUDY

Religious Education among the Jews
Endeavor to find out what religious education Jewish children of the post-exilic period received. What home training did they receive? Did all Jewish children attend the synagogue school? What was the subject-matter taught here? What methods were used in the teaching process? What higher education was there for Jewish youths? Consult J. Klausner's *Jesus of Nazareth.*

Christian Worship and the Synagogue
Study the worship of the synagogue during the pre-Christian era. Note the nature and the chief elements of the Jewish worship. In what respects is our worship like that of the synagogue? What does Christian worship owe to the synagogue? Consult W. O. E. Œsterley's *The Jewish Background of the Christian Liturgy.*

The National and Religious Parties in the Time of Jesus
Look up "Pharisees," "Sadducees," "Essenes," "Zealots," and "Herodians," in your Bible dictionary and in a good encyclopedia. Find out all you can about the history, aims, and influence of each. Consult W. Fairweather's *The Background of the Gospels.*

The Messianic Hope of the Jews
The information given in this chapter is very limited. Endeavor to supplement the material here offered by careful reading on this topic. Consult articles in religious reference books. Consult E. F. Scott's *The Kingdom of God.*

CHAPTER II

THE ORIGIN OF THE NEW TESTAMENT

Bible Readings*—
  Mark 1:1-13—The Threefold Preparation for Jesus' Ministry
  Mark 4:1-20—Jesus' Parable of the Sower
  Mark 6:7-13, 30—Jesus' Disciples on Their First Mission
  Mark 8:27-31—The Disciples' Confession of Jesus
  Mark 9:1-10—Jesus' Transfiguration
  Mark 14:1—16:8—Jesus' Passion, Death, and Resurrection

1. *The New Movement.* In this little land of Palestine, with its varied political, economic, and religious life, Christianity had its birth. In form the Christian movement was a fellowship with a new way of life; it took to itself the name of "The Way" and manifested itself in a spirit and manner of living. This peculiar life, however, did not generate itself. Behind it, underlying it, there was a unique creative power—a divine power which produced the movement, the fellowship, the way of life. This power was the person, life, and work of Jesus, the Christ. Had it not been for him, this Christian movement would never have occurred; it would have been impossible without his divine personality and work.

2. *The New Testament.* Our source of information about Jesus is the New Testament. This body of literature is itself a product of the Christian movement, a product of its life and experience. "The New Testament," says Dr. James Moffatt, "is unintelligible apart from the primitive church." And, since the primitive church is the creative product of Jesus' life and work, it may be said with equal truth that the New Testament is unintelligible apart from the life and work of Jesus. Its writings are flooded with his presence. Their thoughts, their ideals, their enthusiasms, and their worship center in him. The whole movement which we feel in them is the movement of his spirit. It is evident that he is the spring from which flows the rich stream of this new life, as he is the very heart of their testimony.

---
* Note: Bible references for special reading are listed at the head of chapters for the convenience of instructors and students. They are indicated again in the body of the text in **bold type** and should be read in connection with the narrative rather than at the beginning.

There are twenty-seven books in the New Testament: four gospels, one church history, twenty-one epistles, and one apocalypse. While the earliest writings of the New Testament are not the gospels—some of the epistles antedate all the gospels—the order of the books is not without significance; in fact, the order is quite logical: first the records of the marvelous life of Jesus, and then the testimony to the effect of that life. We shall begin, then, with the life of Jesus and its records.

3. *The Career of Jesus.* Measured by human standards, the records of Jesus' life are very meager. Four brief tracts—three of them repeating substantially the same story—tell us all we know of the young Carpenter-Prophet who announced himself the Messiah of the Jewish nation and went about the land preaching the kingdom of God, healing the sick, and teaching men how to live as God's children, until the leaders of the established religion, seeing that the nation was turning to him, conspired to put him to death. The Roman procurator crucified him. But, instead of that being the end of the story, it was but its beginning; for Jesus rose from the dead. The real history of the Christian Church began with that event, for it was this, specifically, that made the church. The church henceforth had a message, and that message was that her Lord had risen from the dead and was alive. This was the testimony of the disciples when the Spirit descended upon them and inspired their marvelous utterances at Pentecost.

4. *The Gospels.* At the head of the New Testament, then, stand the four gospels. This position has been assigned to them because they contain a record of the life and ministry of Jesus Christ, who forms the cornerstone of Christianity. The word "gospel" is the English translation of a Greek word meaning "good tidings." Originally it was applied to Jesus' message (*Mt. 4: 23; Mk. 1: 15*). Then it was used for the message of the apostles (*I Cor. 9: 16*). Very early it came to be applied also to the writings which contained the memoirs of Jesus; Justin Martyr speaks of these writings as "memoirs drawn up by the apostles." The gospels, accordingly, represent the apostolic tradition of what Jesus said and did and suffered. They were naturally placed first in the collection of writings when it was made.

All four gospels found in the New Testament were written

considerably after the middle of the first century—thirty years or more after the earthly life of Jesus had come to an end. Why this delay? Why were they not written earlier? Apart from the very practical hindrance of the cost involved, four reasons have been suggested:[1]

> (1) The first Christians expected the early return of Jesus (*Acts 1:11; 3:20; I Thess. 4:13-18*). This belief was based chiefly on a literal interpretation of Jesus' own words (*Jn. 21:22*), and on the fact that he had not completely fulfilled the Messianic hopes of the Jewish nation. Accordingly, the chief interest of the first Christians would be not in recording past events, but in looking forward to and getting ready for their Lord's return.
> (2) To the first Christians the memory of Jesus' life was so vivid that they did not find it necessary to commit the story of it to writing. To them spiritual communion with their living Lord was the matter of greatest importance.
> (3) When it was necessary to refresh their memories concerning Jesus' life and words, they had Peter and John and James to appeal to. These had been eyewitnesses. So long as the men who had personally known Jesus could travel around among the churches and tell about him out of their personal recollections, there was no great need for written records of his career.
> (4) The first Christians, further, were so thoroughly convinced of the immediate guidance of the Spirit—Jesus' other Self—as not at once to feel the need of written narratives.

The very reasons why the gospels were not written earlier became the reasons why they were written later. Jesus did not return in the flesh. The disciples multiplied. Could those who had not heard Jesus be sure that they had his words? Would it not be well to have a record of them? The first Christians were right in counting the cultivation of the spiritual life, in

---

[1] W. B. Denny, *The Four Gospels and the Christian Life*, Chapter I.

obedience to their Lord's last command (*Acts 1: 4;* cf. *Acts 2: 42*), the chief practical interest in their new fellowship. But those who had not seen Jesus in the flesh—and their number was soon a majority—could not furnish materials for such fellowship from their imaginations. Without an authentic account of what Jesus had done and taught they might drift off into all sorts of vagaries. The church was early confronted with the fact that the eye-witnesses were passing away. Beginning with James, who was put to death by Herod, the men who had seen Jesus and had touched him with their hands (*I Jn. 1: 1*) were falling asleep. Soon they could no longer be appealed to. It was high time to secure their testimony in writing. Already differences were becoming evident in different quarters; Oriental imagination was beginning to embellish the stories of Jesus' life. If there was to be accurate instruction of new converts, some authentic account of "all that Jesus began both to do and to teach" (*Acts 1: 1*) was necessary. The testimony of the apostles must be secured in accurate form. Luke seems to reflect the mind of the young church when he writes in the preface of his gospel:

> "Forasmuch as many have taken in hand to draw up a narrative concerning these matters which have been fulfilled among us even as they delivered them unto us . . . it seemed good to me also, having traced the course of all things accurately from the first, to write unto thee in order, most excellent Theophilus, that thou mightest know the certainty concerning the things wherein thou wast instructed" (*Lk. 1: 1-4*).

But why are there four gospels? This question naturally suggests itself. The number is not without significance, though this came to be seen only gradually, for they were selected out of a number of so-called gospels which were in circulation in the second century. (For example, we read of a "Gospel according to the Hebrews," a "Gospel according to the Egyptians," a "Gospel of Marcion," and a "Gospel according to Peter." A fragment of the last-named was found in Egypt several years ago, and quotations from others are known.) Why then, if there were many "gospels" in circulation, were the four now found in the New Testament selected, and the others allowed to perish? The answer is to be found in the contents of the gospels and in the Spirit's leading of the church's missionary work. **Matthew** had its claims to a place among the sacred writings of the church because it had been used in the training of Jewish Christians. Since it was impregnated with the Old Testament, it was naturally put first. *Mark,* just as plainly, had been written for the practical Romans with their appreciation of dramatic action. The writer of *Luke* had had another group in mind—the great Gentile world. *John,* the latest of the four, represented the deep religious experience of the church in Ephesus. The four gospels thus appealed to four different types of mind. Further, they presented four different aspects of Jesus: Matthew portrayed Jesus as the Lawgiver and King of Israel; Mark pictured him as the Prophet mighty in word and deed; Luke showed him to be the great Humanitarian, touched by the infirmities of all men; and John presented him as the divine Logos (Word) who comes nearer to man in the spirit than in his ministry on earth. It was thus that the four gospels met the four types of mind with which Christianity had to deal. But more remarkable is the fact that they have met the needs of all classes and types of men through the centuries since. *Mark,* with its emphasis on Jesus' ministry of mercy, presents him as the Saviour who has not only "borne our griefs and carried our sorrows" but is the strong Son of God amid all our human ills. *Matthew,* on the other hand, with its emphasis on Jesus as the fulfillment of the Scriptures of his people, presents him as the true and only King of men and the new Law-giver who shows us the way of life. *Luke* meets still another need. It sets forth the story of "the loving Saviour of the world, the sympathetic Friend of all classes and nationalities." Luke's genealogy of Jesus goes back to Adam. His gospel presents Jesus as the world-wide Saviour, "best Lover of men," the Love of God seeking the lost. *John* was addressed to those already claiming to be Christians, a book of meditation and devotion. It deals with the hidden things of Christ's divine nature. It presents "the Saviour for the inner life," the Bread of Life, whereof, if a man eat, he shall never die.

5. *The Relation of the Gospels.* Even a hasty reading of the four gospels will show that, in spite of their differences, the first three are much alike, while the fourth is in a class by itself. *Matthew, Mark,* and *Luke* narrate largely the same events, have nearly the same outline, and use much the same language. For

these reasons these three gospels have been called "the synoptic gospels." ("Synoptic" means "seeing together.")

The first three gospels devote themselves mainly to Jesus' Galilean ministry. The synoptists collect the sayings of Jesus in groups, without much thought of the organic connection between them; John presents the sayings of Jesus in connected discourses. In the synoptic gospels, Jesus is portrayed as a great Wonder-worker whose immediate concern is human need, and he calls himself "the Son of Man"; in John's gospel, the miracles are "signs" of Jesus' divinity, and he is called, and calls himself, "the Son of God." According to the synoptic gospels Jesus conceals his Messiahship even from his chosen disciples until a few weeks before the end of his earthly career; in *John* he is represented as announcing his Messiahship to Nathanael, a stranger, in the first days of his ministry, and as publicly defending it against the Jews. According to the synoptists, Jesus attends but one Passover, that at which he was crucified; according to John he attended three Passovers (*Jn.* 2: 23; 6: 4; 11: 55), and, if the unnamed feast mentioned in *John* 5: 1 was a Passover, four. It is evident that John interprets the synoptic gospels, and that we need all four gospels in order to understand Jesus.

6. *The Gospel according to Mark.* Students of the gospels are agreed that Mark's gospel was the first to be written. This is one of the conclusions which has been reached by the ablest scholars after a century of most devoted study. One of the reasons for this conclusion is this: Practically the whole of Mark's gospel is found in the gospels of Matthew and Luke; out of the 661 verses in *Mark, Matthew* reproduces the substance of 600, and *Luke,* the substance of 350. "Matthew is a fresh edition of Mark, revised, rearranged, and enriched with new material. ... Luke is a new historical work, made by combining parts of Mark with a new story."[2] That is, Matthew took Mark's gospel as a base and added new material to it, while Luke used his new material as a base and adapted Mark's story to it. Naturally, then, if Matthew and Luke used Mark's gospel, his is the earlier document; and John's gospel, it will be shown in another chapter, is later even than Matthew's and Luke's. Therefore it is proper to begin our study of the gospels with *Mark.*

---

[2] B. H. Streeter, *The Four Gospels,* 1930.

The Gospel according to Mark is really anonymous. While the earliest extant manuscripts bear this caption, the text itself tells us nothing about its origin. The testimony of the early Christian fathers, however, is that Mark wrote the gospel, but that it represents the mind of Peter. Papias (about A. D. 125) is quoted in Eusebius' *Church History* as saying: "Mark, having become the interpreter of Peter, wrote down accurately everything that he remembered, without, however, recording in order what was either said or done by Christ. For neither did he hear the Lord, nor did he follow him, but afterwards, as I said, attended Peter, who adapted his instruction to the needs of his hearers but had no design of giving a connected account of the Lord's oracles. So, then, Mark made no mistake, while he thus wrote down some things as he remembered them; for he made it his one care not to omit anything that he heard, or to set down any false statement therein." Some scholars think that the author of the gospel is the unnamed young man who was so nearly arrested in the Garden of Gethsemane, a detail given only in this gospel (*Mark 14: 51, 52*). The references to Mark in the New Testament show how favorably placed he was to get the materials for his narrative. There can be little doubt that Mark was the John Mark mentioned in *Acts 12: 12*. His mother was an influential member of the church in Jerusalem, her house being the place where prayer was made for Peter during his imprisonment under Herod, and to which Peter went after his release. Paul, Peter, and Barnabas were friends of the family. Mark was taken with Barnabas and Paul on their first missionary journey, and, while he disappointed Paul by turning back from Perga (*Acts 15: 39*), nine or ten years later we find him a welcome companion of Paul's during his imprisonment (*Col. 4: 10; II Tim. 4: 11*). Mark was with Peter in Rome during the last days of the apostle's life (*I Pet. 5: 13*). All this supports tradition as to Mark's authorship of this gospel, which is "Peter plus."

Peter's influence has been seen in the following points: (1) the many graphic details, which indicate an eye-witness; (2) the nervous energy of the narrative, characteristic of Peter's temperament; (3) two passages (*Mk. 9: 5, 6* and *11: 21*) which directly reflect Peter's own thought; (4) the fact that the gospel

THE NEW TESTAMENT—A STUDY 33

is written from the standpoint of the Twelve, and, more frequently than Matthew's gospel, from the standpoint of the three honored apostles, one of whom was Peter; (5) the fact that the scope of Mark's gospel corresponds with Peter's statement in *Acts 10:37-41*; (6) the omission of some things creditable to Peter (*Mt. 16:16-19*) and the inclusion of other things not creditable (*Mk. 8:33; 14:30, 68-72*), indicating the influence of Peter. All this supports the tradition that Mark's gospel was based on Peter's preaching.

The same tradition which assigns this gospel to Mark seems to indicate that Mark did not write his gospel until after Peter's death. It was the loss of Peter which prompted the writing out of the memoirs which Mark knew so well. That would place the date after A. D. 65.

7. *Mark's Purpose.* "The chief purpose of the gospel," says Professor Davies, "is to portray the personality of Jesus in such a way that the Church in the hour of its severe trial would receive power to endure and to remain faithful."[3] Mark was writing for days that tried men's souls. It is now generally agreed that his gospel was written for the church in Rome not long after the terrible persecutions under Nero. To divert from himself the suspicion of having set fire to his own city, Nero cast blame upon the hated Christians, charging them with secret vice and with being despisers of the Roman gods and disloyal to Cæsar. Nero inspired the propaganda which made the Christians a hated people, and under his wanton indictment there began "a carnival of blood such as heathen Rome never saw before or since." A "vast multitude"—the phrase is that of the Roman historian Tacitus—were put to death in the most shocking manner. Some were crucified in mockery of the punishment of Jesus; some were sewed in the skins of wild beasts and exposed to the voracity of mad dogs in the arena; some were swathed in pitch-soaked garments, nailed to posts of resinous wood, and burned as torches for the amusement of the Roman mob, while Nero, in fantastic dress, drove his chariot in a mock race by the aid of the gruesome illumination. When the gospel is read with that bloody catastrophe as a background, we see

---
[3] *Abingdon Commentary*, p. 997.

why Mark laid the emphasis he did upon the sufferings of Jesus and the reason for the prominence he gave to his Passion.

8. *The Content of Mark's Gospel.* The material in *Mark* may be divided into three sections:

(1) *Mark 1: 1—7: 23*—Jesus' Public Work;
(2) *Mark 7: 24—10: 52*—Jesus' Retirement;
(3) *Mark 11: 1—16: 8*—The Final Crisis.

In a sense this gospel is a drama in three acts. The first act is the public ministry of Jesus, which divides itself into two parts. In the first part (*Mk. 1: 1—3: 35*) Jesus is presented as the Preacher to all who will hear. The Preacher has a threefold preparation: the ministry of John the Baptist, his own baptism, and his temptation. (**Read Mark 1: 1-13.**) With *Mark 1: 14* Jesus' public ministry is in full swing. Events follow one another in rapid movement. There is the calling of the first disciples, the sensation caused by his authoritative teaching, the violent reaction of evil spirits, the attraction of the multitudes, and the rapid development of hostility on the part of the religious officials. Then apostles are chosen. The second part of the public ministry (*Mk. 4: 1—7: 23*) is marked by Jesus' parable of the sower, which in a way summarizes his own experience as a herald of the Gospel. (**Read Mark 4: 1-20.**) Intensive training of the Twelve is begun, and this is continued in a new campaign against demons and against the reign of death. Finally Jesus sends out the Twelve on their first mission. (**Read Mark 6: 7-13, 30.**) With the beheading of John the Baptist (*Mk. 6: 16-32*) the clouds begin to gather and Jesus withdraws to a desert place. When the Pharisees come upon him with new and intenser fury, Jesus sees that he can prevent his premature end only by withdrawal.

The second act may be called the period of retirement. The withdrawal into the north country is for the further training of the Twelve, until their faith can be brought to the challenge of an open confession. (**Read Mark 8: 27-31.**) After the confession, they behold, in Jesus' transfiguration, his baptism for the cross, and as they follow him now, they realize that the cross is his goal. (**Read Mark 9: 1-10.**)

The third act brings the drama to its climax. In Jerusalem Jesus comes into conflict with the vested powers—the strongly entrenched priesthood. Jesus is overturning the established order; he must go to the cross. His poor broken body is laid in a grave; but the grave cannot hold him. There Mark's drama ends. (**Read Mark 14: 1—16: 8.**)

9. *Characteristics of Mark's Gospel.* This gospel is distinguished by the following marks:

    (1) It is a book of action and of mighty deeds. Mark gives nineteen miracles and only four parables.

    (2) It is a book of graphic detail. The word "straightway" occurs forty-two times.

    (3) It is a book of particulars. Mark likes to use exact numbers. It is this gospel that tells that the temptation lasted forty days; that the woman had suffered with an issue of blood for twelve years; that the apostles were called "the Twelve"; that the disciples went out two by two; etc.

    (4) It has been called a "bi-lingual" book. Mark, having Gentile readers in mind, translates Aramaic words which would not be understood by foreigners; for example: *Boanerges, Bartimœus, Abba, Talitha cumi.*

    (5) It is the most straightforward narrative among the gospels. Mark is no conscious historian like Matthew or Luke; he is less concerned about the literary document he is writing than about the witness he is bearing; even at that, he is but the spokesman of another. His own personality fades out of view; it is Peter who speaks—Peter the downright, outspoken disciple. Peter was no theologian, weaving an interpretation out of patches of fact. Peter was the witness, who could faithfully hand on what he had seen and heard.

The Gospel according to Mark sets forth the faith of the practical Western Church that Jesus Christ is the mighty Saviour of all who come to him in faith.

Questions

1. What new religious movement came into the world at the beginning of our era?

2. What was the creative power of this movement?

3. Where is the record of the beginning of this movement?
4. Why are the gospels placed before the epistles in the New Testament?
5. Why have we only four gospels? Why these four?
6. When was the first gospel written? Why were the gospels not written earlier? Why were they finally written?
7. What name is given to the first three gospels taken together?
8. Contrast the fourth gospel with the first three.
9. Which of the gospels was written first? What is known of its author?
10. What was the chief purpose of this gospel?
11. What are some of its outstanding characteristics?
12. Give an outline of its contents.

Bibliography

Denny, W. B. *The Four Gospels and the Christian Life,* 1925.
Streeter, B. H. *The Four Gospels,* rev. ed., 1930.
Taylor, V. *The Gospels: A Short Introduction,* 1930.
Commentaries:
  Bacon, B. W. *The Beginnings of the Gospel Story,* 1909.
  Blunt, A. W. F. *The Gospel according to Saint Mark,* 1929 (Clarendon Bible).
  Menzies, A. *The Earliest Gospel,* 1901.
  Rawlinson, A. E. J. *The Gospel according to St. Mark,* 1929 (Westminster Commentary).
  Salmond, S. D. F. *St. Mark,* 1922 (New-Century Bible).
Swete, H. B. *The Gospel according to Mark,* 1905.

SUPPLEMENT TO CHAPTER II

Group A—Studies in the Bible

The Beginnings of the Four Gospels
Read, in the following order, *Mark* 1:1-15; *Luke* 1:1—2:7; *Matthew* 1:1-25; *John* 1:1-14. With what event in Jesus' life did Mark begin his gospel? To what point did Luke go for his beginning? How far back did Matthew trace the line of Jesus' family, and can you think of a reason for this? How far back did John go?

Mark's Portrait of Jesus
Read rapidly through the entire *Gospel according to Mark,* noting particularly Mark's picture of Jesus. What kind of Person was Jesus, according to this gospel? Which of the great artists' pictures of Jesus would you select as best illustrating the Jesus of this gospel?

Group B—Topics for Further Study

The New Testament
Look up "Testament" and "New Testament" in an unabridged dictionary and then in a good Bible dictionary or encyclopedia. What information about the New Testament can you glean from these sources? Consult E. F. Scott's *The Literature of the New Testament,* Chap. I.

The Gospels
Look up "Gospel" and "Gospels" in an unabridged dictionary and then in a good Bible dictionary or encyclopedia. What information about the four gospels can you glean from these to supplement the information given in this chapter? Consult E. F. Scott's *The Gospel and Its Tributaries.*

The Synoptic Problem
This is the problem of the relation existing between the first three of our gospels. You will find information in Bible dictionaries, commentaries, and in special works on the gospels. If possible, consult one of the first three books listed under "Bibliography." Make a careful study of this problem. Consult Vincent Taylor's *The Four Gospels: A Short Introduction.*

The Gospel of Martyrdom
This title has been given Mark's gospel. Why? Perhaps you can find out from reading *Mark* itself. B. W. Bacon's *The Beginnings of the Gospel Story* will prove valuable in a study of this topic.

CHAPTER III

THE GOSPELS ACCORDING TO MATTHEW AND LUKE

Bible Readings—
  Matthew 9: 9-13—The Calling of Matthew
  Matthew 5: 1—7: 29—The Sermon on the Mount
  Matthew 21: 23—22: 14—Jesus' Parables of Rejection
  Luke 1: 1-4—Luke's Introduction
  Luke 1: 5—2: 40—Luke's Nativity Stories
  Luke 15: 1-32—Jesus' Parables of God's Love
  Luke 24: 1-49—Luke's Resurrection Stories

The late Professor B. W. Bacon has characterized the *Gospel according to Mark* as, "What the Eye Saw."[1] In it we see the Jesus of public ministry answering the needs of men by his mighty deeds. But there is more to be known of Jesus, and this is to be found chiefly in the two gospels which tell, in addition to what the eye saw, what the ear heard.

1. *The Gospel according to Matthew.* The first of these is the *Gospel according to Matthew,* which is placed first in the New Testament because it links Jesus with the Old Testament; Jesus is presented as the fulfillment of Old Testament Law, Prophecy, and Wisdom. Matthew's gospel has been called "the most important book of Christendom." It was the most widely read gospel in the early church.

The author is indicated in the title—which has preserved the tradition of the early church—as Matthew, who has been identified with Levi. (**Read Matthew 9: 9-13.** Cf. *Mk. 2: 14; Lk. 5: 27.*) Had it not been for his authorship of this book, he would have been one of the least-known of the apostles; for after his call, not a single word or act of his is recorded in the gospels. Some writers, judging from his occupation, think he was a man of means; at least he made a feast for Jesus when he espoused his cause and "forsook all and rose up and followed him." Matthew does not relate this incident himself. Matthew was also probably more accustomed to writing than the other apostles, and he may have made it a practice to write

[1] B. W. Bacon, *Jesus the Son of God,* 1930.

down many of his Master's words. Eusebius, the church historian, quotes Papias as saying: "Matthew wrote the 'words' in the Hebrew dialect and each one interpreted them according to his ability." Later, Matthew's "words" were translated into Greek and built into Mark's narrative, and the total product given the name "Matthew."

There is no clue to the date of writing in the gospel. As its evident purpose was to save Jewish Christianity in a particular crisis—probably one brought on by the fall of Jerusalem in A. D. 70—some scholars place it shortly after that date; others, as late as A. D. 80 or 90.

2. *The Purpose of Matthew's Gospel.* This gospel is addressed to Jewish Christians. Its author's purpose was to show that Jesus is the true Messiah of Old Testament prophecy and that he was divinely commissioned to found a kingdom of believers, based on faith in his Messiahship. We may say that Matthew's gospel is built. (Matthew has been called the architect among the gospel writers.) "His finished work," says Professor Davies, "resembles a massive cathedral, representing the toil of various periods and hands, but withal so deftly harmonized and unified that it gives the impression of a living whole."[2] Some of the stones in this cathedral are the reset testimony of patriarchs and prophets; some, the testimony of Oriental Magi; some, the testimony of shepherds and fishermen, farmers and vine-dressers, children and elders, publicans and sinners; but the testimony of all is that Jesus of Nazareth, true Son of Israel and true Son of humanity, is the Messiah of the kingdom of heaven. The book is written in narrative form, but it is narrative with a purpose—like the historical books of the Old Testament. The aim of the writers of the Old Testament was to show how God's kingdom was realized in the experience of a chosen people and to illustrate the principles on which that kingdom was founded. The aim of the writer of *Matthew* was to show that the kingdom of heaven as proclaimed by Jesus was not something new, but a fulfillment of an old hope. Jesus, the Son of David, is the true Messiah. He and the kingdom were first "offered to the Jews for their acceptance, with warning of the consequences to them of rejection"; and the events leading up to the Passion

---

[2] *Abingdon Commentary,* p. 953.

are so narrated as to show that in the face of this warning they deliberately rejected both the Messiah and the kingdom.

It has been suggested that the immediate purpose of this gospel was to save the faith of Jewish Christians at a particular crisis—possibly, as has been said, the destruction of Jerusalem by Titus. That was a time of fiery trial for Jewish Christians. All the signs of the Lord's return had happened, and yet he had not come. Was it possible that they had deceived themselves and that he was not the Christ? Matthew's gospel is an appeal to all waverers in the faith to trust the King; he might indeed tarry, but he is nevertheless all that Christians have believed him to be. He *is* Israel's hope and the fulfillment of her prophecies—the true Seed of Abraham, the greater Moses, the true Son of David, the final Judge of his people and of the world. The trials which his people were meeting were his trials extended in time; the controversies with the Pharisees in which they were engaged were his controversies continuing on. Let them stand fast, as he stood fast.

3. *The Contents of Matthew's Gospel.* The material of this gospel naturally falls into the following divisions, each ending with the phrase (or its equivalent), "and when Jesus had finished these sayings":

(1) *Matthew 1:1—7:23*—The Kingdom Inaugurated;
(2) *Matthew 8:1—11:1*—The King Invites Followers;
(3) *Matthew 11:2—13:53*—The Growth of the Kingdom;
(4) *Matthew 13:54—19:1*—The King Training His Subjects;
(5) *Matthew 19:2—28:20*—The Passion of the King and Its Consequences.

Matthew begins with a genealogy, which at once relates Jesus with the whole past history of Israel. Throughout the book this linking of Jesus with the prophetic past is evident. Jesus is set forth as the fulfillment of prophecy. His birth is itself such a fulfillment; he is the Immanuel of *Isaiah 7:14*. He has come, a King, and his mission is the establishment of the long-hoped-for kingdom of Israel.

Now comes the preparation for the inauguration of the kingdom in the preaching of John the Baptist and in the baptism and temptation of Jesus. Matthew sees in the baptism of Jesus the fulfillment of all righteousness and the signal for the descent of the inaugurating Spirit, while the temptation marks Jesus' choice of the kingdom of the Spirit over "the kingdoms of this world." Isaiah's prophecies are being fulfilled; even the withdrawal to Nazareth is seen as a fulfillment (*Isa. 9:1, 2*).

Then follow the works of Jesus as Lawgiver, Prophet, and King. Jesus, the Lawgiver, wins his disciples and then, in the Sermon on the Mount, gives them the "better Law." **(Read Matthew 5: 1—7: 29.)** Jesus, the Prophet, as the Servant of Jehovah, of whom Isaiah spoke, heals the sick (*Mt. 8: 16, 17*), and by such mighty works reveals the powers of the kingdom. To extend the kingdom's sway, the Twelve are sent forth (*Mt. 10: 1-42*). The next section (*Mt. 11: 2—12: 50*) shows the attitude of Jesus, the King, to those who question his claims, while, in a long series of parables, the King reveals the secrets of the kingdom, explaining to his followers that he speaks in parables in fulfillment of Isaiah's prophecy (*Isa. 6: 9, 10*). He answers the Pharisees with Isaiah's words, "This people honoreth me with their lips but their heart is far from me." (*Isa. 29: 13*).

As Pharisaic opposition increases, the King retires northward for conference with his followers, and the great confession by Peter is the result (*Mt. 16: 13-20*). The transfiguration is the coronation of the King as superseding the old order (*Mt. 17: 1-12*).

Now follows the announcement of the King that his throne must be the cross, and that the royal vesture is humility. The King is now in Perea on his way to Jerusalem, with the Pharisees snapping at his heels; but the great lessons of self-denial as the law of the kingdom go on. Then, as the conflict deepens, his prophetic denunciation of the Jewish leaders becomes sharper, until, in the open challenge of the triumphal entry and his last parables, he leaves no doubt as to his Messianic claims (*Mt. 21: 1—25: 46*). **(Read Matthew 21: 23—22: 14.)**

Quickly the end approaches. The last division of the gospel contains the story of the death and the resurrection of the King, with especial emphasis on the national guilt in the crucifixion. In all this, Matthew sees the prophetic words of his Hebrew Scriptures fulfilled (*Zech. 11: 13; Isa. 52: 9; Ps. 22: 13;* and others).

4. *Characteristics of Matthew's Gospel.* Some of the outstanding characteristics of this gospel are:

(1) The emphasis placed on the King and the kingdom. The kingdom—the word occurs over fifty times—is its one great theme. This is the kingdom foretold by the prophets.

(2) The constant appeals to the Old Testament, the purpose being to show that the Messianic prophecies were fulfilled in Jesus of Nazareth. There are about a hundred references to the Old Testament.

(3) The large place given to the words of Jesus. These are arranged in systematic form and not broken up into fragments, as in *Luke*. *Matthew* gives the Sermon on the Mount in its most complete form, and fifteen parables, ten of which are found only in this gospel.

(4) The lack of chronological arrangement; Matthew's method is topical. He is interested in subjects rather than in events.

(5) The missionary note. In the genealogy of Jesus, Gentile names are introduced and, contrary to Jewish custom, women are mentioned—Tamar, Rahab, Ruth, and Bathsheba. Magi from the East come to do honor to the infant King. "Many shall come from the East and the West and shall sit down with Abraham, Isaac, and Jacob in the kingdom of heaven" (*Mt. 8: 11*). *Matthew 10* gives Jesus' missionary charge to the Twelve. Here, too, is found the "great commission" (*Mt. 28: 19*).

5. *The Gospel according to Luke.* A great literary critic has called this gospel "the most beautiful book that has ever been written." It won that praise, partly because of its beautiful diction, but more because of the beautiful story it tells. The best introduction to the book is the author's own preface. (**Read Luke 1: 1-4.**) This book is only the first of two volumes of one work—*Luke* and *Acts*—which together carry the story of the Christian movement from the birth of the forerunner of Jesus to the planting of the Christian Church in the Græco-Roman world. The gospel, like *Acts*, is dedicated to "Theophilus," who is addressed as "most excellent," indicating that Theophilus was a Roman official. As Christians did not address one another by such titles, it has been thought that Theophilus was not a Christian but was interested in some public way in the Christian faith. A Dutch scholar has suggested that the gospel and *Acts* were both, in whole or in part, intended as a brief for Theophilus for the defense of Paul before Nero, Theophilus being Paul's counsel or a member of the court which was to hear his case. While that would date this gospel earlier than is generally accepted, it is a very plausible explanation of why *Acts* breaks off without giving an account of Paul's last days.

A second-century tradition ascribes both the gospel and *Acts* to Luke. The author does not himself give us his name in either the gospel or *Acts*, but the above-mentioned tradition says "the third book of the gospel, that according to Luke, was compiled . . . by Luke the physician, when, after Christ's ascension, Paul had taken him to be with him." He is three times named by Paul as his companion in Rome (*Col. 4:14; Philem. 24; II Tim. 4:11*), once as "the beloved physician." In four passages, in which he uses the first person, Luke tells us some things concerning himself (*Lk. 1:1-4; Acts 16:11-17; 20:5—21:18; 27:1—28:16*). These seven passages—the three in the epistles cited and the four in Luke's own writings—contain all that we know about him. Luke intimates that he was not an original witness of Jesus, though he may have known Mary, from whom alone he could have learned of the virgin birth. That he was a cultivated man of literary habits and fine human sympathies and that he knew Greek life and the Greek Old Testament, his writing attests. Beyond this we know nothing of him.

6. *Luke's Purpose and Method of Composition.* The primary purpose of the third gospel is stated in the preface—namely, that Theophilus may "know the certainty concerning things wherein he was instructed." Luke's purpose was to set forth certain facts. He had had many opportunities to learn them— from the women who had ministered to Jesus (*Lk. 8:2; 23:49; 24:10*); from Mary, the mother of Jesus (*Acts 1:14*); from Mnason, an original disciple (*Acts 21:16*); from Philip the deacon (*Acts 21:8, 9*) from whom he had an opportunity to learn about Jesus during a two years' stay at Caesarea (*Acts 24:27*);

from the mother of Mark (*Acts 12: 12, 13*); and from Cleopas (*Lk. 24: 18*). Luke was a man to take advantage of all these opportunities to learn the ultimate facts concerning Jesus. He had his own contribution to make to that story; but that "it might be in order," he wrote the whole story, incorporating Mark's outline and Matthew's "sayings." But to what end? A man does not do a piece of work like this without a strong motive. There is no evidence of personal friendship between him and Theophilus. Luke seems to have known Theophilus only formally. As Theophilus was an official, Luke seems to have set out to show that the Roman Empire had nothing to fear from the Christian religion. "The author emphasizes the fact that Roman officials acquitted first Jesus and then Paul of political crime. If Jesus was crucified and Paul sent in chains to Rome, it was done to please the Jews. Everywhere the Jews are described as the instigators of persecution, and Paul feels sure of justice only when he appeals to the emperor's tribunal."[3] The true story of Jesus with his universal Gospel, Luke believed, would bring the Roman world to its knees before the Christ and it would find in him humanity's best Lover—humanity's Saviour.

7. *The Contents of Luke's Gospel.* The following is the outline of Luke's gospel:

(1) *Luke 1: 1-4*—The Prologue;
(2) *Luke 1: 5—2: 52*—The Birth of the Herald and of the Saviour;
(3) *Luke 3: 1—7: 50*—The Preparation and Early Ministry;
(4) *Luke 8: 1—9: 50*—Extension of the Campaign and the Transfiguration;
(5) *Luke 9: 51—19: 28*—Journeyings toward Jerusalem;
(6) *Luke 19: 29—24: 53*—The Last Days, the Resurrection, and the Ascension.

The gospel begins with angelic announcements of the coming of the herald and of the Saviour. (**Read Luke 1: 5—2: 40.**) Between the angelic announcements are beautiful hymns of faith and hope—hymns which only Luke has recorded. The coming of Jesus is good news—good news of redemption, good news of peace and good will among men, good news especially to the poor.

---

[3] Findlay, *Abingdon Commentary*, p. 1022.

THE NEW TESTAMENT—A STUDY

Then follows the account of the preparation for Jesus' ministry. A sterner note is now introduced: the ministry of the great forerunner, John the Baptist. There is a call for repentance and for a change of life. There can be no entrance into the coming kingdom without a change of heart on the part of all. God's ancient people are no exception. From the officials of church and state down to the multitudes there must be repentance.

Jesus' baptism and temptation are given as in the preceding gospels. In the power of the Spirit, Jesus returns to Nazareth and announces his public ministry in a sermon based on words from *Isaiah* (*Lk. 4: 17-21*). This sermon may be taken as the keynote of Luke's gospel; it is the gospel of good news for the poor. But "no prophet is acceptable in his own country" and so Jesus' fellow-townsmen drive him out of Nazareth. His removal to Capernaum and his early ministry of healing and forgiveness follow (*Lk. 7*).

Jesus now begins to enlarge his circle of operation. He shows himself Lord of nature. He sends the Twelve on their first missionary tour. On their return they are at once led, through their experience of his transfiguration, into the larger meaning of his mission (*Lk. 8: 1—9: 50*).

But soon Jesus' face is set toward Jerusalem. He has need of more fellow-workers; hence the mission of the Seventy (*Lk. 10: 1-24*). The journey to Jerusalem brings out all the rich material crowded into *Luke 11: 1—17: 18*. Parable follows parable—there are twenty in Luke's gospel—emphasizing the value of the lost, and arraigning the narrow position of the Pharisees.

In the last stage of this journey, Jesus develops the doctrine of the kingdom (*Lk. 17: 20—19: 48*) and then enters the last conflict with the religious leaders of the nation. The story of the Passion follows, in line with that of *Matthew* and *Mark*. In his trial and suffering, Jesus is constantly reaching out to strengthen the weak: Peter (*Lk. 22: 31, 32*), the daughters of Jerusalem (*Lk. 23: 28*), the penitent malefactor (*Lk. 23: 43*). Luke gives also the comforting of the women at the tomb, of the disciples on the way to Emmaus, and of the sorrowing disciples in the upper room, to whom he gives a parting commission. (**Read Luke 24: 1-49.**) The gospel closes with Jesus' ascension (*Lk. 24: 50-53*).

8. *Characteristics of Luke's Gospel.* The third gospel has certain marked characteristics, among them the following:

(1) It is the universal gospel. It describes Jesus as the Saviour of all men, the Seeker of the lost among all peoples, the One through whom "all flesh shall see the salvation of God." It is the gospel in which Jesus declares his mission to be "to preach good tidings to the poor"; in which we are told of his association with publicans and sinners; in which the Twelve are charged to preach repentance and remission of sins "unto all the nations." It is in this gospel that we find those parables which strike a universal note: "The Good Samaritan," "The Lost Coin," "The Lost Sheep," "The Lost Son," "The Rich Man and Lazarus," and "The Pharisee and the Publican."

(2) It is the gospel which sets forth most clearly Jesus' way of life. The Christian life is presented not as a peculiar ascetic or ritualistic kind of living, but as a life which recognizes every human instinct and capacity as sacred. It marks out clearly the characteristics of the Christian life. One of these is self-denial. Another is prayer; there are more references to prayer in this gospel than in any other. Luke is equally explicit in his warning against self-deception; he alone gives the parable of "The Vain Excuses," "The Building of a Tower," and of "The Unjust Steward." It is in this gospel that Jesus is most explicit in setting forth terms of discipleship (*Lk.* 14: 26, 27, 33).

(3) It is pre-eminently the gospel for the young. It tells us about the infancy and boyhood of Jesus. It has more words about young men than any other gospel.

(4) It is in a special sense the gospel for women. From first to last more prominence is given to them than in any other gospel. Only *Luke* tells us in detail of the motherhood of Elisabeth and Mary, of Anna the aged prophetess, of the ministering women, of Mary Magdalene, of Mary and Martha of Bethany, and of the women who sympathized with Jesus on his way to the cross.

THE NEW TESTAMENT—A STUDY

(5) But the most characteristic mark of this book is the Gospel of Luke's gospel. No other gospel has made so clear as this one that the Gospel is the good news of God's love. It is in *Luke,* and in *Luke* alone, that we have the three parables of lost things which were restored—the lost sheep, the lost coin, and the lost son. (**Read Luke 15: 1-32.**) These parables present a picture of God's love that we find nowhere else in Scripture. While these parables are the outstanding illustration of Luke's conception of the Gospel, they are not singular. Jesus teaches that God anticipates the needs of his children (*Lk. 12: 30*); that he is concerned about the small details of their lives (*Lk. 12: 7*); that he responds quickly to their cry for help (*Lk. 11: 9-13*); and that he is kind even to the unthankful, and merciful to sinners (*Lk. 6: 35*). Luke's conception of the Gospel is supplemented by his conception of the kingdom of God. As the Gospel is the grace of God freely bestowed, so the kingdom of God is God's rule in the hearts of men (*Lk. 17: 20, 21*). The Pharisees were looking for the signs of the kingdom—physical marks of its presence; Jesus declared that it was already in their midst. It was coming with his ministry—in love and mercy and good will. It was coming in the hearts of men.

Questions

1. Who were the authors of the first and third gospels, and what is known about each?

2. Why was *Matthew* given first place in the New Testament?

3. Contrast the purpose of *Matthew* with that of *Luke.*

4. What are the outstanding characteristics of the *Gospel according to Matthew?* of the *Gospel according to Luke?*

5. What are some things contained in *Luke* which are not found in *Matthew?*

Bibliography

Buttrick, G. A. *The Parables of Jesus,* 1931.
Denny, W. B. *The Four Gospels and the Christian Life,* 1925.
Ramsay, W. M. *Luke the Physician,* 1909.

Robertson, A. T. *Luke the Historian, in the Light of Research,* 1920.
Robinson, W. H. *The Parables of Jesus,* 1928.
Commentaries:
  Adeney, W. F. *St. Luke,* 1901 (New-Century Bible).
  Box, G. H. *St. Matthew,* 1925 (New-Century Bible).
  McNeile, A. H. *The Gospel according to St. Matthew,* 1915.
  Ragg, L. *The Gospel according to Luke,* 1926 (Westminster Commentary).
  Robinson, T. H. *The Gospel of Matthew,* 1928 (Moffatt Commentary).

SUPPLEMENT TO CHAPTER III

Group A—Studies in the Bible

Matthew's Use of Old Testament Prophecy
With the help of a commentary, make a study of the Old Testament quotations found in *Matthew*. Of what events in Jesus' life does Matthew find Old Testament predictions? Consult, if available, Toy's *Quotations in the New Testament,* 1884.

The Kingdom in Matthew's Gospel
Find the passages in *Matthew* which speak of the "kingdom of God," or the "kingdom of heaven." Study these passages carefully. Write a few paragraphs on this topic, setting forth Matthew's view of the kingdom.

The Sermon on the Mount
Study *Matthew* 5: 1—7: 29. Make an outline of the main teachings in this passage. Are there parts especially worth committing to memory?

The Missionary Note in Matthew's Gospel
Read rapidly the entire gospel. Make a list of all passages which have a definitely missionary character or missionary emphasis. What use can you make of these in your church work?

The Hymns in Luke's Gospel
Study *Luke* 1: 46-55; 1: 68-79; 2: 14; 2: 29-32. What names have been given to these hymns? What place have they received in the worship of the Christian Church?

The Humanity of Luke's Gospel
Read the entire gospel, and make a list of all the human interest stories found in it.

The Post-resurrection Stories in Matthew and in Luke
Study *Matthew 28* and *Luke 24*. What common elements do you find in both accounts? What differences are there? How would you explain these differences to one who had difficulties because of them?

Group B—Topics for Further Study

Luke's Accuracy
You will find information on this subject in the introduction of many commentaries. A. T. Robertson's *Luke the Historian, in the Light of Research* and H. J. Cadbury's *The Making of Luke-Acts* will prove very helpful.

Parables
What are parables? Why did Jesus use them? Where did Jesus get the material for most of his parables—from books, from history, from nature, from life, from the Old Testament? Make a list of his parables found in *Matthew* and another of those found in *Luke*. In the light of this study, do you consider it proper or improper to use illustrations from non-Biblical sources in religious education today?

CHAPTER IV

THE GOSPEL ACCORDING TO JOHN

Bible Readings—
John 1: 1-18—John's Prologue: Jesus, God's Word to Man
John 3: 1-21—Nicodemus' Testimony and Jesus' Self-revelation
John 11: 1-45—The Raising of Lazarus—Eternal Life
John 13: 1—17: 26—Last Hours with the Disciples
John 20: 1-31—Jesus' Post-resurrection Appearances

1. *The Fourth Gospel in Contrast with the Synoptic Gospels.* Any thoughtful reader of the four gospels will at once be impressed by the fact that the fourth gospel is in many respects unlike the other three. The very atmosphere is different. "It is as if one had turned from some busy street of the world's life and entered the quiet spaces of a cathedral close.... The green hills and shores of Galilee amid which he has hitherto followed the steps of the Son of Man have to a large extent been changed for the grey courts and precincts of Jerusalem and of the Temple."[1] We feel that we are looking into deeper things. The gospel begins differently. Mark begins his gospel with the ministry of John the Baptist; Matthew and Luke, with the infancy of Jesus; John, with the Eternal Word. In *Matthew, Mark, and Luke,* we are mostly among the hills of Galilee and by the lake bearing that name; in *John* we are at the fords of the Jordan near Jerusalem and the Holy City itself, with but glimpses into the Galilean ministry. In the synoptists, Jesus passes from his baptism to his temptation in the wilderness and seems to remain in retirement until the Baptist's imprisonment; in the fourth gospel, which omits both of these incidents, the Baptist's testimony to Jesus is given immediately upon his appearance and some of John's disciples at once become followers of Jesus.

There is a difference also in the report of Jesus' words. In the synoptists, Jesus' speech is mainly in proverbs and parables; in *John,* he speaks in discourses and lengthy controversies. In the synoptists, the principal theme is the kingdom; in *John,* it is the person of Jesus and life in him. In the synoptists, Jesus

---
[1] Wm. Manson, *The Incarnate Glory,* p. 13.

THE NEW TESTAMENT—A STUDY

hides his Messiahship—even after Peter's great confession (*Mt. 16: 16*) he "charged his disciples that they should tell no man" that he was the Christ (*Mt. 16: 20*); in *John,* he receives Andrew and Peter, as the Messiah (*Jn. 1: 42*), and announces to the Samaritan woman "I am he" (*Jn. 4: 26*). In the synoptists, Jesus lays emphasis on a judgment which is to come at the end of the world; in *John,* judgment is now going on, salvation is a present process, and eternal life has already begun (*Jn. 3: 18, 19; 5: 24*, etc.).

It is evident, then, that there are differences between the synoptic gospels and the fourth gospel. These are determined largely by the differences in the purpose of the synoptists and of John. The synoptists were primarily interested in setting forth the facts of Jesus' life; John had a deeper purpose. (Cf. *Jn. 20: 31* with *Lk. 1: 4.*)

2. *The Author's Purpose.* The church had begun to feel the chill wind of doubt. The primitive beliefs concerning Jesus were being questioned. There were teachers in the church who were treating the gospel history somewhat as a sacred myth. One was saying that it was impossible that God had manifested himself in the flesh. Another was asserting that the taking of our human nature by the Son of God was only apparent. The fourth evangelist was confronted with this type of teaching. The whole matter of Christian faith seemed to be in the balances. Everything turned on the questions: Who was Christ? What was his relation to God and to man? Why should men believe on him? The Greek mind, not entirely satisfied with the Messianic idea presented in the synoptic gospels, wanted answers to these questions. The fourth gospel was written to give answers and to inspire faith in Jesus Christ. The author knew Jesus, but he did not set out to write a record of his words and deeds—that had been done. In his gospel he assumed the other three and did not again delineate what was in them. He had another purpose. He knew that Jesus had revealed himself to be God in true human form; his purpose, therefore, was to make this truth so clear that men might believe in Jesus Christ as the Son of God, and that, believing in him, they might have life through his name. **(Read John 20: 30, 31.)** The scenes depicted, the works done, the words spoken, the observations

made by the writer, are all directed toward the end of enabling the readers to believe that Jesus is the Christ, the Son of God.

That it was the author's purpose to bear this witness, rather than to write a life of Jesus, is plain from the small amount of that life covered by his gospel. Of the 1,000 days of our Lord's ministry, if it covered three years as John seems to imply, this gospel gives an account of but twenty. This in itself is sufficient to set aside the idea that the fourth gospel is just another account of the ministry of Jesus. It is something more: it is the testimony of a witness for a purpose.

3. *Form and Method.* The aim of the fourth gospel, as we have seen, was to bear witness to the divine Sonship of Jesus. How should that witness be borne? As the author of *John* contemplated the ministry of Jesus in the light of the conflicts which the new faith had encountered, he saw that the best and fullest answer to its opponents was the story of the ministry and of the words of the Lord which had made him a believer. He knew how faith in Jesus as the Son of God had grown in his own heart. If the men who were finding such faith difficult could have shared his experience, they would share his faith. He would tell them how that faith had sprung up in him. He had witnessed Jesus' mighty deeds, but they were more than wonders—they were signs of God's eternal glory. He became aware that he was a witness of a new order in human history. The Eternal had come down and dwelt with men, and men were being transformed by that fact. He had seen the process going on from the first day he had been with Jesus. He had seen men changed by contact with Jesus, being made wise by faith or shown as foolish by opposition. Therefore he planned—and the fourth gospel was certainly planned (cf. *Jn. 1: 29* and *Jn. 19: 36*)—the story of growing faith, on one hand, and of growing unbelief, on the other, which had followed the manifestation of the divine glory in the ministry of Jesus.

There is another point. The author had learned the deepest things he knew about Jesus in intimate conversation with him. Jesus' words were life. He revealed himself most fully through them. The author reports Jesus' words as conversation. There is no other book in the New Testament in which we have so much conversation. If the fourth gospel were printed like a modern book, dialogue would form the largest part of it. Repetitions are numerous, as in conversation. The author meant to reproduce the experience which had made him a believer—he had seen, he had heard.

4. *The Fourth Gospel a Personal Testimony.* This gospel professes to be the reminiscence of one who knew intimately and understood the ministry of Jesus. The personal note is more evident than in any of the other gospels. It is present even in the prologue: "We beheld his glory." "This might be taken as the keynote of the gospel," says Professor Iverach. "In all the scenes set forth in the gospel the writer believes that Jesus manifested forth his glory and deepened the faith of his disciples. If we were to ask him, when did he behold the glory of the incarnate Word, the answer would be, in all the scenes which are described in the gospel."[2] He saw that glory in the miracle at Cana, in the night conference with Nicodemus, in the conversation with the woman of Sychar, in the healing of the impotent man, in the feeding of the multitude, in the restoring of sight to the blind man, in the raising of Lazarus, in the washing of the disciples' feet, in the prayer in the garden, in the death on the cross, and in the resurrection. All these are the reminiscences of an eye-witness, together with his reflections on the meaning of what he saw. This witness lives over again the scenes which he describes. He was present on the night in which the Lord was betrayed; he was present in the hall of the high priest; he was present at the cross.

5. *The Author.* Who was the author? The book does not say. "The author did not, like Matthew and Mark, prefix a title to his Gospel" (Zahn). That he was a Jew is manifest. His Greek is in Hebrew idiom. He quotes the Old Testament with a Jew's discrimination. He knew Jewish customs and ritual, even in their unusual details. He used the Judean dating of the Passover, seeming to correct the synoptists as to the time of the last supper. He had a detailed knowledge of Jerusalem and of Palestine. "Whoever the author was," says Dr. Moffatt, "he must have had a first-hand acquaintance with the topography of Palestine prior to A. D. 70."[3] What is more, he has what has been called "an old man's memory for details": the pool

---
[2] *International Standard Bible Encyclopedia,* p. 1723.
[3] J. Moffatt, *Introduction to the New Testament.*

at Bethesda had "five porches"; the lad at the Sea of Galilee had "five barley loaves and two fishes"; Jesus went to Bethany "six days before the Passover"; Jesus "took a towel and girded himself" when he washed the disciples' feet. The minute details of Jesus' arrest, trial, and crucifixion—which are preserved only in this gospel—are further evidence that the account came from an eye-witness.

From the second century the tradition of the church has attributed the fourth gospel to the apostle John. Irenæus, bishop of Lyons (about A. D. 180) speaks of "John the disciple of the Lord, who also lay upon his breast, and who gave out the gospel while he lived in Ephesus." Clement of Alexandria is quoted by Eusebius, the church historian, as saying, "Last of all, John, perceiving that the external facts had been made plain in the Gospels, being urged by his friends and inspired by the Spirit, composed a spiritual Gospel." Origen, of the same city (about A. D. 185-254), who was Clement's pupil, says, "John the Beloved Disciple wrote both the Gospel and the Apocalypse." Thus early the church identified "the beloved disciple" of *John 13: 23; 19: 26; 20: 2* with the apostle John. The likelihood of this identification is increased by the reticence of the writer in the matter of the two pairs of brothers, only one of which he names, who followed Jesus after the Baptist's testimony (*Jn. 1: 35* ff) and in the matter of "the other disciple," who with Peter "entered in with Jesus into the court of the high priest" (*Jn. 18: 15*). No matter whose pen may have finally committed the testimony to writing, the point is this: one who knew Jesus as only "the disciple whom Jesus loved" could know him, bore the original testimony, and the writer of *John 21: 24* was certain that the testimony was true. Accordingly, it was the very words and works of Jesus—words and works which had determined the author's own life and led him to the full assurance of faith—that now saved the church in its first conflict with doubt.

As we read this testimony we are aware that "we are following the line of a great spiritual awakening"—to use the words of Professor Iverach—"and are tracing the growth of faith and love in the life of the writer, until they become the overmastering tone of the whole life."[4] It was the personal testimony of

---

[4] *International Standard Bible Encyclopedia*, p. 1724.

one who was of Jewish origin but whose thought-problems and sympathies were Greek. As *Matthew* was the missionary gospel for the Jewish mind, *John* was the missionary gospel for the Greek mind. "The author of the Fourth Gospel was by general consent a Jew and very probably a Jew of Palestine. But he attempted to present Jesus and his message in some measure as they might have appeared if he, Jesus, had lived and taught in Greek-speaking Asia Minor instead of in Palestine."[5] The writer would have the Gospel do for the cultured Eastern world what it had done for him. He believed that his experience supplied him the key with which to unlock the mystery of the revelation of Jesus to the world. The victory of faith which he set forth was the victory of his own faith. No more likely explanation has ever been given than that this testimony emanated from the apostle John, and that it was committed to writing near the close of the first century.

6. *The Contents of the Fourth Gospel.* The author—probably patterning his work on *Genesis,* which begins with a hymn of creation in which God is put before all things—begins his gospel with a prologue in which the "Word" is identified with this creative God. The remainder of the book traces the twofold effect of the "Word," the divine revelation in Christ, upon men. Some, in faith, receive him; others, in hate, reject him. The author, as has been said, is not concerned to repeat incidents and impressions already set forth in the other gospels; he is concerned to set forth those signs of the glory of the incarnate Word which have inspired and confirmed his own faith, and which he hopes will inspire and confirm faith in others also.

This gospel may be outlined as follows:

(1) *John 1: 1-18*—The Prologue;
(2) *John 1: 19—4: 54*—Dawning Faith;
(3) *John 5: 1—12: 50*—Growing Opposition;
(4) *John 13: 1—17: 26*—The Inner Circle;
(5) *John 18: 1—19: 42*—The Apparent Victory of Hate;
(6) *John 20: 1-31*—The Genuine Victory of Faith;
(7) *John 21: 1-25*—The Epilogue.

The prologue sets forth the author's interpretation of Jesus as the incarnate Word of God. **(Read John 1: 1-18.)** It embodies

---
[5] E. Russell, *The Message of the Fourth Gospel,* p. 21.

his convictions which are the product of a lifetime of reflecting on the significance of the incarnation. Some scholars have seen in John's use of "Word" ("Logos" in Greek) the introduction of a Greek idea; but, as a matter of fact, though John used a Greek term, the idea itself is more closely related to Hebrew than to Greek thought. Already in the Old Testament the Spirit of Jehovah was commonly personified as Wisdom. In Jewish apocryphal books this idea was still more pronounced. Now John saw this idea, so long cherished by his people, realized in the historic Jesus. He saw in Jesus, the Messiah, the One by whom all things were made. But as in creation he had been present, and yet the world had not recognized his presence (*I Cor. 1: 21*), so it was now; "he came to his own, and his own did not receive him. But to as many as did receive him, he gave power to become the sons of God" (*Jn. 1: 11, 12*).

The gospel now traces the historic beginnings of faith in Jesus, by giving the testimony of witnesses: the testimony of John the Baptist, who, when Jesus appears, greets him as the Son of God and the Lamb of God (*Jn 1: 19-36*); the testimony of the first disciples, who, through their spokesman, confess, "Rabbi, thou art the Son of God; thou art the King of Israel" (*Jn. 1: 37-49*); the testimony of the sacramental in life—the first "sign" of Jesus' glory in deed (*Jn. 2: 1-11*); the testimony of Nicodemus (**Read John 3: 1-21**); the testimony of the woman of Samaria and of the Samaritans (*Jn. 4: 1-42*). Throughout this section the faith of many in Jesus is emphasized.

The middle period of Jesus' ministry (*Jn. 5-12*) sees opposition developing among the Jews to the point of persecution. This appears after the healing of the sick man at the pool of Bethesda, which precipitates one of Jesus' sharpest controversies with the Jews and leads him to appeal to divine testimony. The enthusiasm of the people of Galilee and their hopes are dashed by Jesus' refusal to allow himself to be made king (*Jn. 6: 15*). This is followed by the withdrawal of many of his disciples (*Jn. 6: 66*). At the Feast of Tabernacles there is much murmuring concerning him (*Jn. 7*). Jesus openly charges the Jews that they seek to kill him. While opposition is growing, faith too is being developed and deepened (*Jn. 6: 67-69; 8: 28-30*). The healing of the man born blind (*Jn. 9*) precipitates another controversy. At the Feast of Dedication the Jews seek to stone

Jesus because he insists that he and the Father are one (*Jn. 10: 22-31*). Then Jesus retires beyond the Jordan and here he is acclaimed as the Christ, and a large addition is made to the number of his disciples. Here he prepares his followers for his last great sign, the raising of Lazarus, by which many of the Jews are led to believe on him. **(Read John 11: 1-45.)** Only six days of his life remain, but they are momentous days, and nearly one-half of the gospel is devoted to their events. They are marked by a growing faith on the part of the people, but also by a deepening hatred on the part of their leaders. Jesus, therefore, decides to offer himself to the nation as the Messiah, thus bringing matters to the issue which he knows will result in his crucifixion (*Jn. 12*).

Before the Passover, Jesus takes the inner circle of his followers into the upper room in Jerusalem and opens once more his inmost heart to them. Some of the most precious gems of the gospel are preserved in these chapters telling of Jesus' humility, his farewell discourses, and his intercessory prayer. **(Read John 13: 1—17: 26.)** It was in this ministry of the inner sanctuary that Jesus disclosed himself to his disciples as one with the Father and the Holy Spirit. Here we witness brooding love on the part of the Master and deepening faith on the part of the disciples.

In his account of the last days of Jesus, John seems to follow the synoptists, but he does something more; he shows, from inside knowledge, that Jesus' crucifixion was due to the hatred of the priestly hierarchy, of which Pilate was forced to become the unwilling agent. He passes by the agony in Gethsemane—he had already taken his reader into the inner sanctuary of the upper room—but he is careful to indicate that Jesus, once arrested, does not get out of the hands of the priestly party until they have secured the indictment of their Sanhedrin with which to arraign him before Pilate. His being taken first to Annas and then to Caiaphas is but a pretext by which to gain time to summon the Jewish court, which could not sit before daylight. John's picture of Pilate is that of a weak man whose sins as procurator left him unfree to deny the demands of "the rulers of the Jews." The one sublime figure in the dark picture is Jesus, who defies the priests, pities Pilate, and comforts his disciples. Then the cross becomes his throne. Finally Joseph of Arimathea and Nicodemus yield a tardy allegiance.

John's account of the resurrection seems supplementary to the narratives of the synoptists; its selection of appearances is made on spiritual principles to illustrate the triumph of the risen Lord in the faith of his disciples. Bishop Westcott has pointed out that, amid a diversity of details in the resurrection narratives of the four gospels, there is agreement in certain outstanding particulars: (1) The appearances were made only to believers; (2) They were determined by the Lord's purpose; (3) They were received with hesitation at the first; (4) No mere report was accepted; (5) The revelation issued in a conviction of the reality of the resurrection. The fourth gospel lays stress on the victory of faith in Peter and John (*Jn. 20: 8*), in Mary (*Jn. 20: 16*), in the eleven and their company (*Jn. 20: 20*), and in Thomas (*Jn. 20: 28*). (**Read John 20: 1-31.**)

The book closes with an epilogue (*Jn. 21*). This chapter is commonly described as an appendix, an addition of a later date, and perhaps of a later hand. The purpose of the addition seems to be to confirm the impression that "the disciple whom Jesus loved" was John.

7. *Points to Be Remembered.* The following facts about the fourth gospel are worth remembering:

    (1) The fourth gospel is a book of testimony. We have in turn the testimony of the Baptist (*Jn. 1: 19-36*), of the first disciples (*Jn. 1: 35-51*), of Nicodemus (*Jn. 3: 1, 2*), of the Samaritans (*Jn. 4: 42*), of the works of Jesus (*Jn. 4: 54—5: 9*), of Jesus' own words (*Jn. 7: 16, 28*), of the apostle John (*Jn. 19: 35*), and of the witnesses of the resurrection (*Jn. 20: 8, 16, 20, 28*). Professor Bacon has called this gospel "The Gospel of What Entered into the Heart of Man."

    (2) The fourth gospel is the gospel of the divine Sonship (*Jn. 20: 31*). As the central thought of *Mark* is Jesus the Prophet of the kingdom; of *Matthew*, Jesus the Messiah; of *Luke*, Jesus the Saviour of man; so, of *John* it is Jesus the Son of God.

    (3) The fourth gospel is the gospel of the humanity of Jesus as over against the Docetists, who denied it.

(4) The fourth gospel presents man's life as a battleground between two worlds, light and darkness, faith and unbelief, love and hate.
(5) The fourth gospel is the gospel of eternal life (*Jn. 3: 3; 5: 24; 6: 28*). Eternal life is a living, present possession, not merely a future contingency.
(6) The key words of the fourth gospel are "believe," which occurs 99 times; "life," which occurs 34 times; and "love," which occurs 31 times.
(7) The fourth gospel is the gospel of the presence of Christ. The Lord had not returned "in like manner as ye [the disciples] have seen him go up into heaven." In the course of time the faith of many Christians began to give way. One of the objects of the fourth gospel was to suggest to its readers that the Lord is present with those who believe.
(8) The fourth gospel transformed the current beliefs concerning death, judgment, and future life. Instead of merely looking forward to a judgment at the end of the world, the presence of the Son of God, either awakening faith or provoking unbelief, is also a present judgment. The change in life wrought by faith is present salvation; the state of soul when faith is refused is present condemnation. The change from unbelief to faith—which is passing from death to life—is present resurrection. The possession of the salvation which faith secures is present eternal life.

Questions

1. What are some of the outstanding differences between the synoptic gospels and the fourth gospel?
2. Who, according to the tradition of the early church, is the author of the fourth gospel? What are some of the difficulties in the way of accepting this authorship? How may these difficulties be overcome?
3. What was the author's main purpose in writing his gospel?
4. What does this gospel add to our knowledge of Jesus gained from the synoptic gospels?
5. What are some points to be remembered about this gospel?

Bibliography

Manson, Wm. *The Incarnate Glory*, 1923.
Russell, E. *The Message of the Fourth Gospel*, 1932.
Scott, E. F. *The Historical and Religious Value of the Fourth Gospel*, 1909.
Strachan, R. H. *The Fourth Gospel: Its Significance and Environment*, 1917.

Commentaries:
  Bernard, J. H. *Critical and Exegetical Commentary on the Gospel according to St. John*, 1929 (International Critical Commentary).
  Lenski, R. C. H. *Interpretation of St. John's Gospel*, 1931.
  Macgregor, G. H. C. *The Gospel of John*, 1928 (Moffatt Commentary).
  McClymont, J. A. *St. John*, 1922 (New-Century Bible).

SUPPLEMENT TO CHAPTER IV

Group A—Studies in the Bible

John's Prologue
  Study carefully John 1:1-18. What was John's conviction concerning Jesus Christ? What does this truth mean to you?

"Life" in the Fourth Gospel
  Look up the word "Life" in a concordance. Note the references to it in John. Study these passages carefully. Write a few paragraphs on the topic as stated above. Consult E. Russell's *The Message of the Fourth Gospel*.

"Love" in the Fourth Gospel
  Follow the suggestions given under the preceding topic, substituting "Love" for "Life."

The Prayers of Jesus in the Fourth Gospel
  Study John 11:41, 42; 12:27, 28; 17:1-26. What can you gather from these passages as to the character and spirit of Jesus' prayers? May we think of the church as praying these prayers?

The Testimony of Others to Jesus
  Study the following passages carefully and note the impressions various persons had of Jesus, as expressed in their testimony: **John 1:19-36; 1:35-51; 3:1, 2; 4:5-42; 9:1-38; 20:11-16; 20:24-28.** Write

THE NEW TESTAMENT—A STUDY

a paragraph or two expressing your own personal convictions concerning Jesus.

Group B—Topics for Further Study

The Relation of the Fourth Gospel to the Synoptic Gospels
Consult articles in Bible dictionaries, encyclopedias, and commentaries. If a harmony of the gospels is available, study it. Make a list of items found in *John*, but not found in the synoptics.

The Value of the Testimony of the Fourth Gospel
The fourth gospel grew out of deep Christian experience. Its testimony is of a high order. What does this testimony tell us concerning Jesus Christ? What value has this teaching for us? Consult C. E. Raven's *Jesus and the Gospel of Love*, 1931. Is it enough simply to translate the teachings of Jesus into another language? What did John do? What was his method of bearing testimony?

CHAPTER V

THE LIFE AND TEACHING OF JESUS

Bible Readings—
   Luke 2:41-50—The Boy Jesus in the Temple
   Matthew 3:1-17—Jesus' Baptism
   Luke 4:1-14—Jesus' Temptation
   Luke 4:16-22—Jesus' First Sermon in Nazareth
   Matthew 17:1-13—Jesus' Transfiguration
   Mark 11:1-11—Jesus' Triumphal Entry
   Luke 22:14-20—Jesus' Institution of the Lord's Supper
   John 19:1-42—Jesus' Death
   Mark 16:1-8—Jesus' Resurrection

We are now ready to gather together the elements of the life and teaching of Jesus as given by the four gospels and to articulate them into a single whole.

THE LIFE OF JESUS

1. *Jesus' Birth and Early Years.* Only two gospels, *Matthew* and *Luke,* tell of Jesus' birth. According to their narratives, Jesus was born in Bethlehem sometime before 4 B. C. (the date of Herod's death), during the reign of Cæsar Augustus, the first Roman emperor. *Luke* notes the detail that the census which took Joseph and Mary to Bethlehem was in the days of Quirinius, governor of Syria. *Matthew* records a visit of Magi from the East—men of a Persian cult renowned for their skill in interpreting dreams and in astrology—who had found in the heavens a sign of the birth of a great Western king. The Parsees believed that the coming of a great hero was heralded by the appearance of an unusual star, as was the birth of Alexander the Great. There are known to have been notable conjunctions of planets during the years 8-6 B. C. In this story of the coming of the Magi the Babe of Bethlehem is seen as the magnetic Power who would draw unto himself not only the Jews but also the Gentiles, and as the King who would overthrow the star-deities of the East.

Both *Matthew* and *Luke* give genealogies which trace the lineage of Jesus through David to Abraham. Luke's genealogy traces it still farther back, to "Adam, who was the son of God." The lists differ. It is plain that Matthew wrote from the viewpoint of Joseph, and Luke, from that of Mary. According to both writers, Jesus was "conceived by the Holy Ghost." At the time of his conception and birth, divine revelations of the coming of Christ were given to Elisabeth, the mother of John the Baptist; to a little group of shepherds; and to aged saints in the Temple.

On the eighth day, the Babe was circumcised (*Lk. 2: 21*), and his name was called "Jesus"—the Greek form of "Joshua," meaning "Saviour" (*Mt. 1: 21*).

The coming of the Magi having roused the fear of Herod, Joseph, after a divine warning, took the young Child and his mother to Egypt (*Mt. 2: 13-15*), whence he was brought to Nazareth after Herod's death.

2. *Jesus' Youth.* Of Jesus' childhood we know only what *Luke* tells us (*Lk. 2: 40, 52*). Since Joseph was a carpenter, Jesus' home was that of an artisan; Jesus himself was later called "a carpenter" and "the son of a carpenter." His training as a Jewish child would include the learning of sections of the Law as well as of the prophets. The incident in the Temple, when, at the age of twelve, he had been taken to the Passover, discloses him as a Child of remarkable spiritual acuteness. **(Read Luke 2: 41-50.)** Luke narrates the incident to show that Jesus was where he felt he belonged.

After this visit to Jerusalem he returned to Nazareth, and, for an unnamed period of years, was subject to Joseph and Mary. There is no sign of any acquired knowledge in the mind of Jesus except what he might have got in his home and in the synagogue. Though he was surrounded by Greek culture, there is no trace of it in any of his words. He was trained in no other schools than those of his people. So far as is known, Jesus, up to the time of his public ministry, lived in Nazareth. He was a simple, country Workingman, patiently bearing the limitations of his class. If tradition has preserved the true site of Mary's home and Joseph's shop, Jesus' nights were spent in a windowless cave-hut, with the family and the domestic animals; and his days were spent—except when he worked away from home—in a windowless cave-shop, lighted only from its entrance. He knew both the work and the worries of a laboring man's life, the pinch of poverty, and the anxiety of unemployment; but he knew also the satisfaction of work well done, the strength that comes from self-support, and the joy of lifting burdens from others' shoulders.

3. *Jesus' Preparation and Early Ministry.* Jesus entered upon his ministry in the midst of a period of national excitement. While in Galilee a revolutionary movement of the Zealots was growing and gathering the momentum which finally resulted in the destruction of Jerusalem in A. D. 70, an exclusively religious movement was attracting many in the Jordan region of Judea. While the revolutionists were urging people to resist taxation, John the Baptist was urging them to repent of their sins (*Mk. 1: 4, 5*). John and Jesus were second cousins through their mothers, but there is no evidence that they had ever met before their meeting at the Jordan. Jesus was drawn to John's baptism as he was drawn to the Temple—through religious interest. John was saying the things Jesus was thinking. The kingdom of God was at hand and the Messiah was coming to establish it. The religious leaders of the people were hypocrites and the people themselves, self-satisfied. What the nation needed was righteousness of the sort demanded by the old prophets. A new Israel must be made, such as God could accept and use. The ceremony of admission to this new Israel was baptism. Jesus came to that baptism, not, as it appeared, as a penitent to be absolved from sin, but as a candidate for service in the new commonwealth which John was preaching. He had a great spiritual experience and knew that he was the Son of God, called to proclaim God's kingdom. (**Read Matthew 3: 1-17.**)

Jesus' baptism was followed by his retirement into the wilderness of Judea where he was subject to those fundamental temptations which come to everyone called to a spiritual mission; only he met them with the fuller equipment of his spiritual power. The tempter being vanquished, *Luke* tells us that "Jesus returned in the power of the Spirit into Galilee." (**Read Luke 4: 1-14.**) But the fourth gospel gives us a connection between the ministry of John and the ministry of Jesus. According to the fourth gospel they began their work side by side in the Jordan valley, and several of John's leading disciples passed from John's company to Jesus'. When Jesus went to Galilee he was accompanied by four disciples, themselves from Galilee, and there he showed his first "sign" (*Jn. 2: 1-11*) and won additional disciples. He sojourned at Capernaum for a time and

Important Places in the Life of Jesus

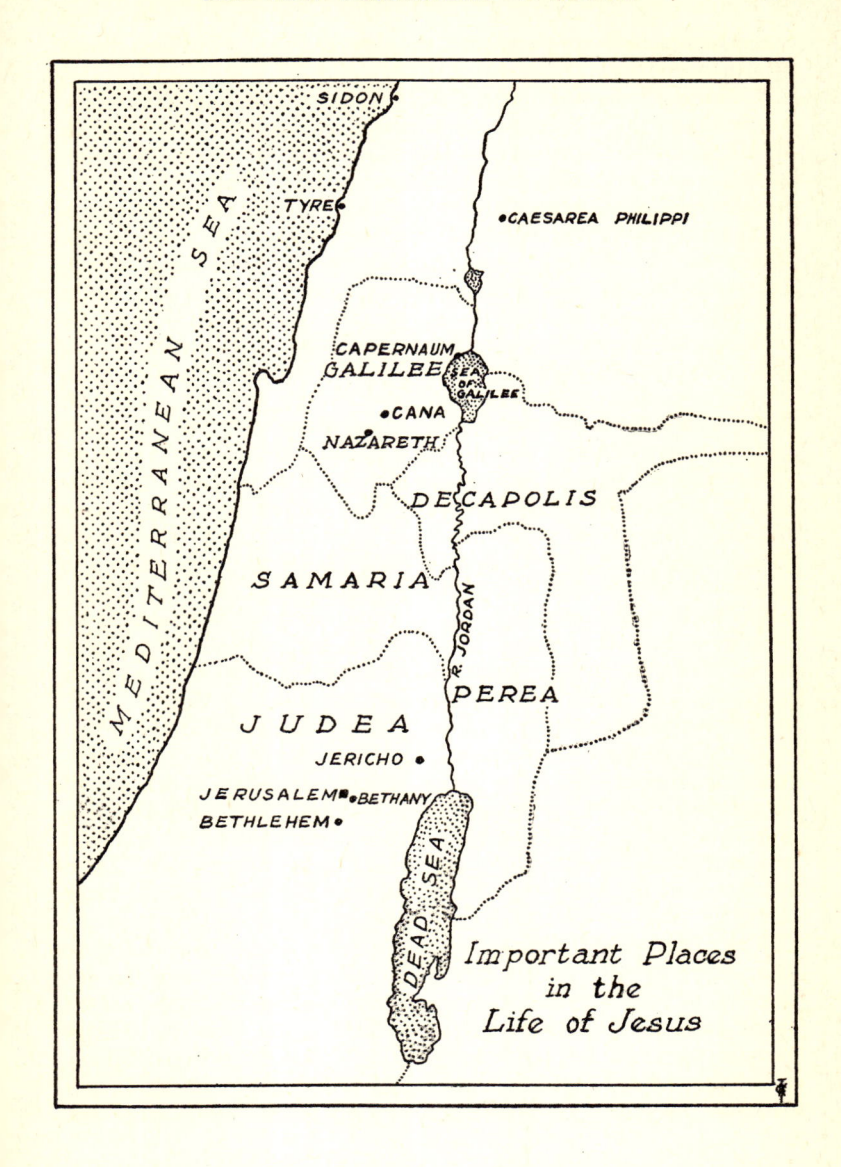

then went up to Jerusalem to attend a Passover Feast. His ministry there brought him into conflict with the religious authorities, and this opposition continued up to his death. It was to escape a premature crisis—for Herod Antipas had imprisoned John (*Mt. 4: 12*)—that he withdrew, first into the country of Judea and then into Galilee (*Jn. 3: 22; 4: 1-3*).

4. *Jesus' Galilean Ministry.* Jesus had now come into full consciousness of his mission, and it was in Galilee, his own country, that he formally offered himself as the Prophet of the kingdom of God. (**Read Luke 4: 16-22.**) This was a period of preaching and healing (*Mt. 4: 23*); a period of miracles[1] (*Mk. 1: 29-34*); a period of conflict with the powers of evil, and the result was that the demons were subject to him (*Mk. 3: 11*). In his kingdom disease is to have its cure.

Capernaum now became the center of Jesus' ministry (*Lk. 4: 31*). His fame went abroad and great multitudes followed him. His teaching began to stand out prominently, and he was recognized as One who spoke with authority. In Galilee, with its revolutionary mind, he did not proclaim himself a "Son of David" Messiah, but adopted a title of deeper significance, calling himself "the Son of Man." His teaching led him to organize the Twelve as apostles, and these he sent out on a missionary tour, which was the beginning of their own work in his name (*Mt. 10*). In this period, also, began the serious opposition of the Pharisees, who were offended because he "ate with publicans and sinners." It was to these Pharisees that Jesus made the great declaration of his mission (*Mt. 9: 12, 13*). The fourth gospel explains the crowds which were in motion by recalling that they were Passover pilgrims, this being the second Passover mentioned in Jesus' ministry.

The fourth gospel and the synoptics come together at the feeding of the five thousand in the region east of Galilee, which was the occasion of Peter's first confession (*Mk. 6: 34-44; Jn. 6: 1-69*).

5. *Jesus' Retirement.* Scribes and Pharisees now sought him out more boldly. His claim of power to forgive sins, his teach-

---

[1] Jesus' miracles were predominantly miracles of healing. Dr. Klausner has shown how the terrible history of Palestine in that period of almost continuous war which had just preceded would have produced an inordinate amount of misery and disease—particularly, mental disorders. All this Jesus associated with the hostile power of Satan, the enemy.

ing concerning holiness (holy life, holy food, holy days), and his mingling with "sinners" caused them to look upon him as a heretic. Jesus was more and more thrown back upon the Twelve, and it became evident that he was training them for the future. The murder of John the Baptist by Herod and Herod's threat against Jesus were followed by Jesus' withdrawal from public work in Galilee. It was evident that he could not trust the popular nationalism to understand his mission and purpose. Hence, taking the Twelve with him, he went north to the region around Tyre and Sidon, seemingly making a circuit outside the boundaries of Herod's tetrarchy to the region of Decapolis (*Mk. 7:24-31*). Crossing the Sea of Galilee to Dalmanutha, he at once encountered fresh opposition from Jerusalem, so that he recrossed the lake to return to the neighborhood of Cæsarea Philippi, where Peter, rising above Jewish patriotism, confessed him to be the Christ of God (*Mt. 16:15, 16*). Here, too, occurred Jesus' transfiguration. **(Read Matthew 17: 1-13.)** Following the transfiguration we are struck with a new note in Jesus' ministry—the note of urgency. He is urgent to have the kingdom proclaimed and sends forth the seventy (*Lk. 10*), while he pours forth his evangelistic parables in rapid succession. He is impatient of Pharisaic quibbling (*Lk. 11, 12*). He is urgent about his own witness at Jerusalem and takes the open road through Perea and Judea. He no longer walks with his disciples in easy converse but in front of them, under great strain (*Mk. 10:33*). He speaks openly of his death, picturing his end in terms of the Suffering Servant (*Isa. 53*) who was rejected and slain. Thus he pressed on to Jerusalem.

6. *Jesus' Passion and Death.* The arrival at Jerusalem began with a tumultuous welcome, which Jesus deliberately accepted. **(Read Mark 11: 1-11.)** This welcome was no doubt due chiefly to the Galilean peasants present at the Passover, although the raising of Lazarus from the dead (*Jn. 11:1-45*) had had an electric effect on the Passover pilgrims. The cleansing of the Temple followed, and a revolution might have ensued, had Jesus been willing to accept the role of nationalist leader and to proclaim himself a "Son of David" Messiah. His last public discourses, reported by Matthew (*Mt. 23-25*), were a heartbreaking farewell to the nation that had rejected him, while his last private discourses, preserved by John (*Jn. 13-17*), were a

warm and intimate farewell to his disciples. In the shadow of his betrayal, Jesus instituted his Supper. **(Read Luke 22: 14-20.)** His enemies, however, were confederated in a league of hate—the Pharisees because of his attitude to the Law and his, to them, blasphemous claims; and the Sadducees because of his attitude to the Temple—and, with the timely help of Judas, succeeded in getting him away from his followers and arraigning him before Pilate. The indictment—preserved by Luke alone (*Lk.* 23: 2)— was a threefold charge of treason: (1) he was an agitator; (2) he urged the Jews not to pay the imperial taxes; and (3) he claimed to be a king. Pilate could not ignore such a charge. In the test of strength with the procurator, the Jews won, and Jesus was crucified as a malefactor. Joseph the Arimathean offered his tomb; Nicodemus brought a costly mixture of spices; and the body of Jesus was buried with more care than had ever been accorded it in life. **(Read John 19: 1-42.)**

7. *Jesus' Resurrection and Ascension.* Thus ended the earthly life of Jesus of Nazareth; thus began the Christ of the Christian Church. That Jesus rose from the dead all four gospels and all the New Testament attest. Eleven appearances to his disciples are recorded: (1) to Mary (*Jn.* 20: 11-18); (2) to the women (*Mt.* 28: 9); (3) to Peter (*I Cor.* 15: 5); (4) to the two disciples on the road to Emmaus (*Lk.* 24: 13-32); (5) to the Eleven, Thomas being absent (*Jn.* 20: 19-25); (6) to the Eleven, Thomas being present (*Jn.* 20: 26-29); (7) to the seven disciples by the sea (*Jn.* 21); (8) to the Eleven on a mountain in Galilee (*Mt.* 28: 16-18); (9) to the five hundred brethren (*I Cor.* 15: 6), possibly identical with "(8)"; (10) to James (*I Cor.* 15: 7); (11) to the disciples on Olivet (*Lk.* 24: 50-53). What these appearances attest is that Jesus won the victory over death, is alive, and that his followers have in his resurrection the sign and seal of the forgiveness of their sins and enjoy a communion with him more continuous and vital than when he was in the flesh. **(Read Mark 16: 1-8.)**

Forty days after his resurrection, Jesus ascended to heaven (*Acts 1: 9-11*).

THE TEACHING OF JESUS

Jesus was a teacher with a vital message. His object was to announce and to inaugurate the kingdom of God. The background of his teaching was the Old Testament, which had ministered to his personal needs (*Mt. 4: 4, 7, 10*), had furnished the prospectus of his ministry (*Lk. 4: 16-19*), and had given him the key to the Messiahship (*Mk. 9: 11-13*). He knew the covenant Law of Israel, but he knew also the traditions of the elders—the body of minute, artificial precepts with which the authoritative teachers of the Jews had burdened the people. Against these burdensome laws, Jesus' spirit rebelled. He came to preach deliverance. He taught, therefore, not as the scribes. He had his own method. He was original; his message was fresh; and the people heard him gladly.

8. *Jesus' Method.* Jesus left no writing. His teaching was all done by direct discourse. His method was to give "seed-thoughts"—principles from which applications could be made for all times and all places. These principles were expressed in several ways.

We probably have the original type of Jesus' teaching in the synoptic gospels. Here he is shown as teaching by proverbs, as, for example, in that collection of sayings which we call the Sermon on the Mount. This discourse is largely proverbial in form. A proverb is an expressed or implied simile and is the simplest form of comparison. Proverbs are elemental words of wisdom, principles of life and conduct, and are very effective in that they are easily held in memory. Those who heard Jesus would have little difficulty in remembering what he said.

Jesus used also parables. A parable is an expanded proverb; that is, a truth is stated in a story form of comparison. Twenty-eight parables have been preserved in the gospels. They are of different kinds, many of them being analogies of the spiritual world drawn from the life of men or from the processes of nature. All of them are meant to reveal or illustrate some phase or principle of the kingdom of God.

Jesus taught, too, by his wonderful deeds. These, in themselves, were channels through which he made truths known. Further, much of Jesus' explicit teaching was the interpretation of his deeds. The fourth gospel has preserved several such interpretations. In such cases, Jesus' deed was the "sign," or the simile, while Jesus' words made the application. Thus the feeding of the five thousand suggested the discourse on the living bread (*Jn. 6: 1-58*); the healing of the man born blind, the discourse on the Good Shepherd (*Jn. 9:1—10:16*); the raising of Lazarus, the discourse on eternal life (*Jn. 11:1-46*).

In all his teaching, Jesus showed originality; that is, his teaching grew out of his own religious experience. His was not a mind which had been molded in the schools of the rabbis. The one book that he knew was the Scriptures of his people. Jesus quoted nothing beyond it; he quoted it as his authority, but in his use of it he transformed and spiritualized it. The idea of God was not a book-truth with him. He had an inner experience of God, and it was that which was the source of his life and teaching. His soul was aflame with the will of God. What he found God to be, in this inner communion, produced the great passion of his life—his passion for the kingdom of God.

9. *The Content of Jesus' Teaching.* Naturally, then, *the kingdom of God* became a first subject of Jesus' teaching. Old Testament prophecy had come to an end, leaving the ideal of God's kingdom an unfulfilled hope. Jesus took up the message of the prophets where they had left off, but he interpreted the kingdom ethically. To Jesus the kingdom is the rule of God's beneficent will in the hearts and lives of men. It is not, therefore, a material thing whose coming can be discerned by the physical eye; it is a spiritual relation between man and God, and then between man and man. The kingdom, according to Jesus, is not something which man creates, but a sphere of privilege and blessedness into which man is graciously admitted, in which he becomes a worker with God—a privilege for which all else is to be sacrificed (*Mt. 6:33; Lk. 10:22; Jn. 17:3*). It is a kingdom of grace, whose message is "good news" (*Mt. 4:23; Lk. 2:10*). While its blessings are offered to all who hear the gospel, not all find admission. The conditions of entrance are repentance and faith (*Mk. 1:15; Lk. 7:50; 13:3, 5*). Repentance means a change of mind (including the will); faith means complete surrender of the will in a new loyalty. Within the kingdom the rule of God is manifest in righteousness in the hearts of its members and in their relation with each other and with the world.

In this interpretation of the kingdom, Jesus opposed two prevalent ideas. The Pharisees advocated a separation from the common interests of life by a ritual observance which made those who kept it a peculiar people of God. Jesus opposed this idea. He held that it was not external cleanliness or observance or even abstinence that made men righteous; this externalism led mainly to hypocrisy. Again, Jesus opposed the idea of the nationalists, whose hope was military revolution and the violent overthrow of the Roman government. He held that this was not the way to the kingdom.

The "Sermon on the Mount" is Jesus' platform of the kingdom. It is a proclamation of other-worldliness in this world. Throughout his teaching he states that selfishness must be overcome; that righteousness, love, and forgiveness must prevail; that prayer, humility, purity, equity, honesty, and loyalty to himself must find a place in men's lives. The kingdom, in Jesus' teaching, is the great unifying principle in life. Its supreme and constraining motive is love (*Mt. 22: 39, 40; Mk. 12: 28-34*). In relation to God this attitude expresses itself in a spirit of dependence and trust; in relation to man, it shows itself in mercy, forgiveness, active beneficence, and the shining light of a good example.

A missionary motive, therefore, animates the kingdom. The spirit of the kingdom manifests itself to others in loving service. It tries not only to meet the expressed needs of others (*Mt. 5: 42*), but even to anticipate them (*Mt. 7: 12*). Like God's love, it takes the initiative. This explains the self-sacrifice of the members of the kingdom.

The kingdom is to come through the preaching of the Gospel, which is to be sown as seed in men's hearts (*Mt. 13: 3-9*). Hence the preaching of the Gospel of the kingdom is the mission of the church (*Mt. 28: 19, 20*). This kingdom within men's hearts cannot be seen; it can be known only by their transformed lives (*Mt. 7: 16*). There will be many disappointments in the missionary work of the kingdom. The lowly will come more rapidly than those in high places (*Lk. 14: 16-24*). Many will come into the church who are not part of the kingdom (*Mt. 13: 47-49*). But the kingdom will come, and the reward of the faithful will be an abiding place in it (*Lk. 22: 31, 32*).

A second subject of Jesus' teaching was *the Fatherhood of God.* Underlying all his words about the kingdom is the thought of God as Father. The Father makes the sun to rise on the evil and on the good, and sends rain on the just and on the unjust (*Mt. 5: 45*); the Father feeds the birds of the air and clothes the lilies of the field (*Mt. 6: 25-30*); the Father forgives his wayward children (*Lk.* 15:20); the Father knows men's needs (*Lk.* 12:30). Men are to pray to their Father who seeth in secret (*Mt.* 6:6). It is to the Father that Jesus will commend his faithful disciples (*Mt.* 10:32); it is not the will of the Father that any of them shall be lost (*Mt.* 18:14); it is to the Father that Jesus prays for them (*Jn.* 17).

A third subject of Jesus' teaching was *his own Messiahship.* There were two types of expectation among the Jews who looked for the Messiah: (1) the expectation of the coming of "the Son of David"—a view of the Messiah which went back to the prophets; and (2) the expectation of the coming of "the Son of Man"—a view which was held by a small circle of Jews as early as the time of the writing of *Daniel* (*Dan.* 7:13, 14). Jesus spoke of himself as "the Son of Man," a title which he deliberately used to draw attention to himself as the Messiah in the broadest sense, for to him the Son of Man was the heir of all human experience, whose glorification lay on the other side of humiliation and death. Jesus thus transformed the popular idea of the Messiah by linking it—and therefore himself—with the idea of the Suffering Servant of *Isaiah 53.* The Jews never connected these two—the Suffering Servant and the Messiah— and even to the Twelve this idea proved a stumbling-block. But with Jesus it was central. "The influence of this great passage of Scripture [*Isaiah 53*] upon the mind of Jesus," says Canon Box, "can hardly be measured."[2] After his transfiguration, Jesus constantly held before the Twelve the fact that the Scriptures had announced that "the Son of Man" must suffer many things. "In the background of all our Lord's teaching," says Bishop Gore, "is the secret, disclosed to the disciples, and finally to the world, that he, the Son of Man, is really the promised Messiah, who is to be rejected, is to suffer, is to die as a sacrifice for his people, and only so finally to be raised to glory."[3] Because he fulfills this service for men he can invite all in physical and spiritual distress to cast their burden upon him. The Son of Man has power to forgive sins (*Mk.* 2:5), to give rest to the weary and heavy laden (*Mt.* 11:28), to speak with final authority about God (*Jn.* 8).

---

[2] Box, *The People and the Book,* p. 454.
[3] Gore, *A New Commentary on Holy Scripture,* Part II, p. 276.

Jesus spoke of himself also as "the Son of God"—and that in a unique sense. He did not put his own Sonship in the same category with that of others; he spoke of "my Father," "the Father," and "your Father," but never of "our Father" (except in the Lord's Prayer, which was not a personal prayer, but a prayer to be used by his disciples). It is clear, then, that Jesus had a unique consciousness of his own relationship with God.

A fourth subject of importance in Jesus' teaching was *sin and its forgiveness*. Jesus saw the human world as a sinful world, needing to be redeemed (*Mk. 7:15*). The Old Testament stressed sacrifice as necessary for redemption, and this necessity had led to a system of animal and vegetable offerings. These the prophets had challenged as in themselves unavailing, while the great prophet of *Isaiah 53* had found the true sacrifice in the Suffering Servant. Jesus interpreted the Suffering Servant as himself. He was, therefore, to give his life a ransom for many. In the sacrament of the Lord's Supper he speaks of the new covenant in his blood made for the remission of sins. It was a vicarious act, but it was not to remain an objective vicarious act, but was to make itself manifest in the transformed life of the believer. In *John 3* Jesus told Nicodemus that for entrance into the kingdom of God a new birth is necessary. This regenerating power is also the gift of God (*Lk. 11:13*), who is like a watchful father always ready to receive the returning penitent (*Lk. 15:20*). He has gifts for the sustenance of the new life which he gives through the eating of his sacrificial body and the drinking of his outpoured blood.

A fifth note in Jesus' teaching centered in the idea of *the church*. He declared that faith in him would beget a new relation—a fellowship of faith, a "body of believers." This is brought out in his response to Peter's confession at Cæsarea Philippi: "Thou art Peter, and on this rock I will build my church." Here he grouped all those who shared Peter's faith, in one body. It was in this church, the true faithful remnant of God's people, that Jesus instituted the sacrament of his Supper.

A sixth thought which found a place in Jesus' teaching was *eternal life*. Eternal life, according to his teaching, is life lived in relation with God. That is what Jesus came to give men (*Jn. 5:24*). This life does not terminate with the death of the body (*Jn. 11:25*). Jesus affirmed a life beyond the present and taught a resurrection of the body. He looked forward to his own resurrection (*Jn. 2:19*), and he promised the resurrection of those who shared his life (*Jn. 6:54*). There are many questions we should like to ask which Jesus did not answer. Jesus does not satisfy our curiosity, but he has satisfied our needs. He was concerned rather to give men right ideas of God and of their relation to life here and now than to unveil the future.

Questions

1. What can you tell of:
    (1) Jesus' infancy, childhood, and youth?
    (2) Jesus' preparation for his ministry?
    (3) Jesus' public ministry?
    (4) Jesus' Passion and death?
    (5) Jesus' resurrection and ascension?
2. What methods did Jesus use in his teaching ministry?
3. In what six subjects did the greater part of Jesus' teaching center? Which of these occupied the chief place in his teaching?
4. What was Jesus' conception of the kingdom of God? What views of the kingdom did he reject?
5. What did Jesus teach concerning:
    (1) God?
    (2) Himself?
    (3) Sin and forgiveness?
    (4) The church?
    (5) Eternal life?
6. What does Jesus mean to you?

Bibliography

Barton, G. A. *Jesus of Nazareth: A Biography*, 1926.
Denney, J. *Jesus and the Gospel*, 1907.
Hayes, D. A. *The Heights of Christian Blessedness*, 1928.
Hayes, D. A. *The Heights of Christian Living*, 1926.
Hayes, D. A. *The Resurrection Fact*, 1933.
Headlam, A. C. *Life and Teaching of Jesus the Christ*, 1923.
Kent, C. F. *The Social Teachings of the Prophets and Jesus*, 1917.
Scott, E. F. *Ethical Teaching of Jesus*, 1926.

Smith, D. *The Days of His Flesh*, 1910.
Stalker, J. *The Life of Jesus Christ*, 1891.

SUPPLEMENT TO CHAPTER V
Group A—Studies in the Bible

The Parables of Jesus
  With the help of a Bible dictionary, make a list of Jesus' parables. Read these parables and note after each the main truth which it contains. G. A. Buttrick's *Parables of Jesus* will prove helpful.

"The Father" in Jesus' Teaching
  Look up Jesus' use of "Father" as applied to God. What was Jesus' relation to the Father? What was the Father's attitude toward men? What did the Father do for men? What does the Father expect of men? Write a few paragraphs on Jesus' conception of the Father.

"The Kingdom of God" in Jesus' Teaching
  With the help of a concordance, study selected passages on "the kingdom of God" and "the kingdom of heaven." Confine your study to Jesus' own teachings. How do your findings compare with the position taken in this chapter?

Social Principles in the Sermon on the Mount
  Study *Matthew 5:1—7:27* and *Luke 6:20-49*, and make notes on the social principles found in these sayings of Jesus. Endeavor to state these principles in modern terms.

Group B—Topics for Further Study

The Life of Jesus as an Example
  In what sense was Jesus "the first Christian"? Wherein is he our example? How can we imitate him? Think through his life; then, in a few paragraphs, answer these questions.

The Influence of the Old Testament on the Teaching of Jesus
  Make a study of Jesus' references to the Old Testament. Note what Old Testament truths he made his own. G. H. Gilbert's *Jesus and His Bible* will be a valuable aid in this study.

The Teachings of Jesus and the Life of Our Times
  Study again the section of this chapter dealing with the teachings of Jesus. What values have these teachings for our life today?

Consult the article on "The Life and Teachings of Jesus" by E. E. Fischer in *A Commentary on the New Testament.*

The Social Teachings of Jesus
Consult C. F. Kent's *The Social Teachings of the Prophets and Jesus* and E. F. Scott's *Ethical Teachings of Jesus.*

CHAPTER VI

THE CHURCH IN PALESTINE

Bible Readings—
Acts 2:1-47—The Descent of the Holy Spirit and Its Effect
Acts 3:1—4:31—Conflict and Courage
Acts 6:1-7—A Church Problem and Its Solution
Acts 8:5-17—The Gospel in Samaria
Acts 8:26-40—A Convert from Africa
James—An Early Christian Tract

As the four gospels are our primary sources of information concerning the work of Jesus, so *The Acts of the Apostles* is our primary source of information concerning the movements of the primitive Christian Church or rather, of the two great leaders of the church, Peter and Paul. Light is, of course, thrown upon the character of the Christian movement, by the epistles; but it is in *Acts* that we have the main outline of the church's early history.

1. *The Acts of the Apostles.* The seed had been sown; how did it grow? The gospels describe what Jesus "began both to do and to teach" in his personal ministry; *Acts* describes what Jesus continued to do and to teach through his church.

This book is one of the finest pieces of narrative writing in the New Testament. Its author, it seems certain, was Luke, the writer of the third gospel (*Acts 1:1*). His aim was, evidently, to tell the story of the growth of the church from Jerusalem to Rome in such a way as to show that this growth was the continued work of the ascended Christ. He possessed three sources of information: (1) the testimony of living witnesses; (2) the records of local churches; (3) his personal observations. His personal observations are clearly seen in certain passages in which he uses the first person plural—the "we sections"—(*Acts 16:10-17; 20:5—21:18; 27:1—28:16*). They are evidently extracts from the travel diary of an eyewitness. A careful study of Paul's traveling-companions shows that only Luke and Titus were with him at all the points mentioned in these passages. In other words, Luke was there. Further, the author tells us that he collected the testimony of others who had a part in the early history of the church. Scholars now acknowledge that the author was a careful writer—the accuracy of many details, lately confirmed by discovered inscriptions, is proof of this—and that his account is reliable.

Acts divides itself into two major parts:
  (1) *Acts 1-12*—The church in Palestine;
  (2) *Acts 13-28*—The church in the Roman Empire.
In the first part the central figure is Peter; in the second, Paul.

2. *The Church in Jerusalem.* The narrative of *Acts* begins with Jesus' ascension. The Lord's last command to his disciples was that they should wait for the descent of the Holy Spirit and then be his witnesses in Jerusalem, Judea, Samaria, and the uttermost parts of the earth (*Acts 1: 8*). Accordingly, the Eleven, with a group of others, including the mother of Jesus and his brethren, waited in the upper room for the coming of the Holy Spirit. During this interval of waiting, a successor to Judas was chosen (*Acts 1: 15-26*).

On Pentecost—a festival commemorative, in later Judaism, of the giving of the Law—the Holy Spirit came upon the church, accompanied by a sound as of a rushing, mighty wind and an appearance of cloven tongues like as of fire. Wind and fire were, in Hebrew thinking, agents of generation and purification. These were, therefore, fitting symbols of the Holy Spirit. An explanation of this marvelous phenomenon was, naturally, required. It was Peter's task to offer the interpretation of it. His sermon was something more than an explanation and interpretation, however; it was the declaration of the Spirit-filled church that the promised Spirit of Jehovah, predicted by Joel, had come, and that he had been sent by Jesus, the God-approved, risen, and exalted Messiah. This testimony to Jesus was followed by a practical appeal to the hearers to repent and accept Jesus as Saviour and Lord, and by baptism to become members of the new Israel, of which Pentecost was the beginning. The appeal was effective; the response was tremendous. (**Read Acts 2: 1-47.**)

Thus a new fellowship came into being—the Christian Church. To the outside world, it appeared simply as the formation of a new sect within Judaism. These believers in Jesus continued to participate in the worship of the Temple and to observe the Law. But they also had their own meetings, which were marked by four distinguishing characteristics: (1) they had a creed, the center of which was Jesus, who was soon to return to them as the glorified Lord and Master; (2) they had a fellowship in which all were considered "brethren"; (3) they observed the Lord's Supper; and (4) they united in common prayer, the very breath of their fellowship. They looked on themselves as a new creation; they lived in a new world; and, like their Lord, they increased in favor with God and man.

So long as the church remained "indoors" and contented itself with its fellowship and prayers, it was not disturbed. It was only when it became missionary and militant that it provoked opposition. The first opposition came when Peter, having healed a lame man, insisted that the cure had been wrought by the power of Jesus. Peter and his companion, John, were twice arrested and released, the second time, however, only after receiving a severe flogging. But, in spite of this opposition, the church prospered. **(Read Acts 3: 1—4: 31.)**

Thus far no practical problem had arisen within this young church. The fellowship was under the direction of the apostles, whom Jesus himself had trained. It was they who taught, directed the worship, and administered the sacraments. But now a problem arose. The membership of the church contained a considerable number of poor persons whose needs had to be met. With great unselfishness, the better-circumstanced members shared their possessions with the needy. The work of distribution was done by the apostles. In the course of time, however, the Greek-speaking Jews of the fellowship complained that "their widows were neglected in the daily ministration." The apostles, realizing that their primary work was preaching, called the church together and suggested the selection of qualified men for this practical service of ministering to the poor. The suggestion met with approval and seven men were set apart for the work. **(Read Acts 6: 1-7.)**

One of the seven men selected for this service was Stephen. He was more than an administrator of poor-funds; he was a synagogue preacher of great power. In his synagogue disputations, he laid himself open to the charge of speaking against the Temple and of undermining the Law; and that touched not only the Sadducean priests but also the Pharisees, who up to this time had been benevolently neutral with regard to the Christian movement. Once aroused, however, they were a dangerous foe, for they had the support of the people. Little had the apostles dreamed, when they had appointed the seven deacons from among the Grecians (Hellenistic, or Greek-speaking Jews) that they were opening the door to the Gentiles and, consequently, to a crisis within the church. Stephen's teaching, as has been said, laid him open to the charge of undermining the Law. His more conservative brethren were offended, and lodged charges against him in the Grecian synagogue of which he himself was a member; but his accusers were no match for him—"they were not able to resist the wisdom and spirit by which he spoke." Defeated in argument, they now resorted to false witnesses and had Stephen arraigned before the Council on the twofold charge of speaking against the Law and against the Temple.

Stephen's defense was an interpretation of Jewish history which cut the ground from beneath his opponents' smug confidence. He told them that God had had a purpose in the call of the Israelite nation, which they had both missed and forfeited. That purpose was independent of the land, the Temple, and the Law. Their ancestor Abraham had been called out of a heathen land; there had been no Temple until the time of Solomon, and, even after its establishment, prophets had declared that "the Most High dwelleth not in houses made with hands"; and, further, God's covenant was earlier than and independent of the Law. Accordingly, God's original purpose was independent of the land, the Temple, the Law. But—meeting his accusers on their own ground—though their Law had been given by the mediation of angels, they had from the first disobeyed it. Their Law pointed to the coming of a new and greater prophet, a second Moses, who should supersede it; he had come, but they had put him to death. It was, therefore, not he, but they— such was the implication—who were the law-breakers. They were betrayers and murderers.

The result was inevitable. In a fit of frenzy, "they cast him out of the city and stoned him." That day there "arose . . . a great persecution against the church which was in Jerusalem," and the disciples "were scattered abroad throughout the regions of Judea and Samaria, except the apostles" (*Acts 8:1*). But as a storm scatters the seed far and wide, so this persecution scattered the seed of Christian faith; for wherever the disciples went, they preached the Word. The ultimate effect of Stephen's martyrdom was, therefore, the extension of the witness of the church. Hitherto the Gospel had been preached largely by the apostles; now it became the testimony of scattered believers. The circumstances into which they were thrown would inevitably make them tell the story of Jesus; they had to explain why they were driven from their former homes. Informal testimony soon became more formal preaching, and in this way new centers of the Christian movement were developed (*Acts 8: 1-4*).

3. *The Church in Samaria.* The Lord had promised his disciples: "Ye shall receive power, after that the Holy Spirit is come upon you; and ye shall be witnesses unto me both in Jerusalem, and in all Judea, and in Samaria, and unto the uttermost part of the earth." Gradually this promise was being fulfilled. The Spirit was leading the disciples into the field of their inheritance. The church had made a beginning of witnessing in Jerusalem; persecution had driven it into other parts of Judea; and now it was carrying its testimony into Samaria. The agent of evangelistic work in Samaria was Philip, the second of the seven deacons. The people of Samaria were a despised people. They were neither Jews nor Gentiles, and yet in a sense they were both. Jesus himself had said that he had not been sent except to the lost sheep of the house of Israel (*Mt. 15: 24*), but he had gone to the Samaritans. And now the Spirit was using these same Samaritans as "a sort of half-way house from those in the covenant to those who were outside it." To these Samaritans, then, Philip preached Christ, and many of them believed and were baptized. Hearing of the progress of the Gospel in Samaria, the apostles at Jerusalem sent Peter and John to follow up Philip's work, and their approval was shown by their confirming the converts with the laying on of hands—the beginning of the church's rite of confirmation. (**Read Acts 8: 5-17.**)

From Samaria, Philip was directed by the Spirit to take the road toward Gaza, an old Philistine city. Like Abraham, he set out, not knowing whither he went. The road was a lonely desert way, but it chanced to be the way by which an Ethiopian officer was returning from Jerusalem to his native land. From the fact that he had been to Jerusalem to worship and was reading the Hebrew Scriptures, it would seem that he was a proselyte, a convert to the Jewish faith. Philip had an unmistakable call to join himself to him and to interpret to him the passage—*Isaiah 53: 7*—which he was reading. This gave Philip an opportunity to speak of Jesus Christ. The Ethiopian was convinced of the truth of Philip's testimony, confessed his own faith in Christ, and asked to be baptized. Philip readily consented; and thus a new Christian witness went to Africa to testify for the Gospel. Philip then continued his work in other parts of Palestine. **(Read Acts 8: 26-40.)**

4. *The Epistle of James.* Some scholars are of the opinion that the *Epistle of James* was inspired by this early dispersion of the church. It was addressed to "the twelve tribes which are scattered abroad," from which it may be taken that the church still centered in Jerusalem, and that the letter, or tract—for it is more a tract than a personal communication—was written to meet the needs of Jewish Christians who had been scattered by persecution. Its contents fit equally well in the period of the Domitian persecution. **(Read James.)**

Who wrote it? The epistle itself states that it was written by James. There are at least three Jameses in the New Testament. James the son of Zebedee, one of the Twelve, was put to death by Herod Agrippa in A. D. 44. James the son of Alphæus was also one of the Twelve, but there is no indication that he was connected in any way with the scattered Jewish Christians addressed in this letter. More probably the author is the James mentioned in *Acts 15: 13*, known as "James the Just," a brother of Jesus, who, according to Eusebius, "was wont to go alone to the sanctuary, and used to be found prostrate on his knees so that they grew hard and worn like a camel's." Jesus' brothers had not at first believed in him (*Jn. 7: 5*) and none of them was found among the apostles. But after the resurrection, Jesus appeared to James (*I Cor. 15: 7*), and thereafter he and his brothers associated themselves with the apostles (*Acts 1: 13, 14*). His relationship to Jesus and his own character made him the leader of the church in Jerusalem.

One other possibility remains: that a writer in a later persecution wrote in the name of James. Whoever he was, the writer of this tract was a downright man, who was accustomed to say what he thought—a man of strong convictions and fearless expression. He was not a theologian. He was interested less in doctrine than in life. He hated sham of any kind and his indignation boiled over upon any form of hypocrisy. Mere orthodoxy of faith to him seemed dangerous; orthodoxy of life he considered more essential. His position on faith (*Jas. 2: 14-26*), however, must not be regarded as opposed to faith as such; his opposition was against mere dead professions, against empty lip-faith. Though James emphasized the social aspects of the Gospel, he also recognized that the way Christians behaved in the wider relationships of life depended upon their moral inwardness: "Cleanse your hands—purify your hearts—humble yourselves in the sight of the Lord" (*Jas. 4: 8, 10*). Where there is not this inwardness of religious purpose, there is no hope of a commensurate outward life. Evidently, rich men and men of rank had begun to seek church honors. James was as merciless with them as Micah had been (*Jas. 5: 1-6*); he feared their influence upon the poor, for he realized that the poor often give wealth a false rating by their attitude to it (*Jas. 2: 1-9*). He warned sharply also against railing tongues, the spirit of strife, and evil desires (*Jas. 3: 1—4: 17*). All these things were obstacles to true brotherhood, and to James the Christian community was a brotherhood.

As has been said, this tract was written during a period of persecution; those who believed in Jesus were suffering heavy trials. James saw in these trials an opportunity for growth in Christian character. Accordingly he urged Christians to rejoice, to be patient, and above all else, to hope—to hope for the certain coming of their Lord (*Jas. 5: 7-11*).

The following is a summary of the contents of this epistle:

(1) *James 1: 1-15*—An Exhortation to Patience;
(2) *James 1: 16-27*—The Marks of True Religion;
(3) *James 2: 1-13*—Respect of Persons;
(4) *James 2: 14-26*—Faith and Works;
(5) *James 3: 1-18*—The Responsibility of Teachers;
(6) *James 4: 1-17*—The Worldly versus the Christian Life;
(7) *James 5: 1-20*—Rich Tyrants—The Need of Patience and Prayer.

Questions

1. What is the main source of our knowledge of the development of early Christianity? Who was the author of this source? Where did he get his information?

2. How did the Christian Church come into being?

3. What was the relation of the first Christians to Judaism?

4. What led to the break with Judaism?

5. What was the immediate effect of Stephen's martyrdom?

6. Trace the extension of the church during and immediately after this period of persecution.

7. Which New Testament book may have been written at this time? What can you tell about this book and its author?

Bibliography

Cadbury, H. J. *The Making of Luke-Acts,* 1927.

Robertson, A. T. *Luke the Historian, in the Light of Research,* 1920.

Scott, E. F. *The Beginnings of Christianity.*

Commentaries:

   Blunt, A. W. F. *The Acts of the Apostles,* 1926 (The Clarendon Bible).

   Gilbert, G. H. *Acts,* 1908 (Bible for Home and School).

   Jackson, F. J. F. *The Acts of the Apostles,* 1932 (Moffatt Commentary).

SUPPLEMENT TO CHAPTER VI

Group A—Studies in the Bible

The Beginnings of the Church

   Make a careful study of *Acts 1: 1—8: 40.* Outline in detail the story of the church's development.

The Speeches in Acts 1-8

   Study the speech of Peter to the Pentecost multitude (*Acts 2: 14-40*); of Peter to the people on the porch of the Temple (*Acts 3: 12-26*); of Peter to the Jewish rulers (*Acts 4: 8-12* and *5: 29-32*); of Stephen before the Council (*Acts 7: 2-53*). What are the elements common to all?

The Epistle of James
>Make a thorough study of the entire epistle. Note particularly all points that have practical teaching values for our day. Keep a list of these, with their Biblical references.

Group B—Topics for Further Study

The Historical Value of Acts
>Consult H. J. Cadbury's *The Making of Luke-Acts*, A. T. Robertson's *Luke the Historian, in the Light of Research*, and W. Ramsay's *The Bearing of Recent Discovery on the Trustworthiness of the New Testament*.

The Communal Movement of the Apostolic Church
>Contrast with the Marxian Communism of Soviet Russia. Consult Kent's *The Social Teachings of the Prophets and Jesus*.

The Early Organization of the Church
>Consult in *A Commentary on the New Testament*, edited by H. C. Alleman, the article on "The Beginnings of the Christian Church," by A. R. Wentz.

The Hellenists
>Midway between Judaism and Romanism stood Greek culture, or Hellenism. It was the culture of the Roman world. What service did it perform for the early Christian Church? Consult encyclopedias and Bible dictionaries. Consult also S. Angus' *The Religious Quests of the Roman World*.

CHAPTER VII

THE EXTENSION OF THE CHURCH TO THE GENTILES

Bible Readings—
Acts 9:1-9; 22:4-21; 26:8-18—Saul's Conversion
Acts 10:1-48—Preparation for the Gentiles
Acts 11:19-26—The Growth of the Church in Antioch
Acts 13:1—14:28—The First Foreign Missionary Tour
Galatians—An Epistle on Christian Freedom

The Christian Church had its beginning within the Jewish community, but the new wine soon burst the old wine-skins. The new faith, founded on the resurrection of Jesus, though opposed by Sadducees and Pharisees, was making progress. From Jerusalem as a center, the Christian movement was spreading through Judea and Samaria, and even beyond these territories. Already there were evidences, too, that other than Jews were being impressed with the new Gospel. The admission of Hellenists and Samaritans into the church gave promise of an ultimate extension of the Gospel to the Gentile world.

For the great work of carrying the Gospel to the nations a fit and effective instrument was needed. Where was he to be found? There were many missionaries bearing testimony to their Lord, but there seemed to be no one to undertake this great and untried task. Meanwhile, however, the Spirit was at work, and that in a most unlikely quarter. From the beginning, Christianity had recruited followers from the ranks of its foes. Of all these foes, the arch-persecutor, by his own confession, was Saul of Tarsus. By an amazing experience, he was to furnish the church with the instrument it needed.

1. *Saul of Tarsus.* Saul, later called Paul, the most influential personality to espouse the Christian faith in the entire history of the church, was a Jew of Tarsus, a large and important city of southeastern Asia Minor. It was "no mean city." It was the capital of the province of Cilicia, and the seat of a university famous for its Stoic school of philosophy. Here the mystery cults were practiced. Close to Tarsus was the home of the poet

Aratus, whom Saul quoted in his address on Mars Hill. It was also a commercial port, a transshipping point between the East and the West. Saul was, therefore, a city-bred boy, as Jesus had been a country-bred Boy, and he continued to be "city-minded." His figures of speech are from the market place and the arena, just as those of Jesus were from the farm and the village.

Of Saul's family and early training, next to nothing is known. He never refers to his parents. There is a casual reference to a sister (*Acts 23: 16*) whose son did Paul a service in Jerusalem when his countrymen sought his arrest. As a boy he learned the trade of tent-making; it was probably the trade of his father. His chief schooling was, naturally, at the Jewish synagogue school. The language of instruction was Greek, and the Septuagint was his Bible. But he learned also to read the Old Testament in Hebrew.

Another advantage which Saul had for his work among the Gentiles was his Roman citizenship—an uncommon distinction, for, it must be remembered, relatively few of the inhabitants of the empire were honored with citizenship status. How his family had obtained its Roman citizenship we do not know. Ramsay suggests that his family had been planted in Tarsus with full citizenship rights as a part of a colony settled there by one of the Seleucid kings in order to strengthen his hold on the city. Or, citizenship may have been presented to Saul's father or grandfather for distinguished services to the state. But, however he came into its possession, it proved a boon to him in his career. It was his Roman citizenship which made possible his appeal to Cæsar (*Acts 25: 11*); to it also probably was due the possession of the Latin name *Paulus,* which is uniformly used after he began to appeal to the Græco-Roman world (*Acts 13: 9*); and to it he must have owed not a few of the privileges which made his ministry in Rome a success.

Nature had given Saul a keen and vigorous mind; his speeches and letters reflect an endowment of high order. Nature had also given him an acquisitive spirit. It was probably his keen ambition for an education that led to his being sent to Jerusalem in his boyhood. At the age of fifteen he became a student of Gamaliel, the great Jewish rabbi of the school of Hillel (*Acts 22: 3*). Jerusalem and its great Temple fascinated him, and he became, as he himself tells us, "exceedingly zealous for the traditions of his fathers" (*Gal. 1: 14*).

How long Saul remained in Jerusalem at this time is not told, but it was a long enough period for him to become thoroughly trained in all that would have made him a rabbi. He had mastered the Scriptures of his people; he knew "the traditions of the elders"; and he believed that God had revealed himself in their history and experience in a full and final revelation of truth. He knew the strength of Judaism, and he had learned the arguments which the Jews used against the Christian faith. He himself learned to use those arguments. And later, after his conversion, he was able to sympathize with Jews who found it difficult to renounce their ancestral religion, but he knew also why they should give up the old for the new.

2. *Saul's Conversion.* Saul first comes into the New Testament picture with the martyrdom of Stephen, the beloved deacon. Stephen's address enraged young Saul, as it did the other members of the Jewish Council, for he "consented to his death" and he guarded the garments of those who stoned Stephen. The scene fired the young zealot's mind with the determination to exterminate the new heresy, and he became a vigorous persecutor of the church. He went the length of making house-to-house search for Christians, dragging out men and women and delivering them to prison. His name became the terror of Christian homes, and such was his reputation among his colleagues that the Sanhedrin appointed him a special agent to stamp out the Christian heresy in Damascus.

Suddenly, like a bolt from the sky, a thing happened which changed Saul's career. The story of Saul's conversion is told three times in *Acts:* the first is the account of Luke (*Acts 9: 1-18*); the second is Paul's own story as he told it to the mob which later threatened his life in Jerusalem (*Acts 22: 4-16*); the third is the account given in his defense before Agrippa (*Acts 26: 9-18*). Paul refers to it also in *Galatians 1: 15, 16* and in *I Corinthians 9: 1*. The outstanding fact in each account is the appearance of the living Jesus. Saul was sure that he had seen the Lord and that therefore he was no less a witness of Jesus' resurrection than Peter and James and all the other apostles to whom the risen Christ had appeared. He always looked upon this experience as constituting his call to the apostleship. **(Read Acts 9: 1-9; 22: 4-21; 26: 8-18.)**

A great change took place in Saul. He refers to it in *Galatians 1: 11-17,* where he speaks of a Providence which had been working, even from his birth, to prepare him for his ministry to the Gentiles and which culminated in the inner revelation which gave him the Gospel direct from the Lord. After his vision, Saul was led to Damascus, and there he was welcomed as a brother in Christ by Ananias and then baptized into the Christian faith. Immediately he sought out the Jewish synagogues and preached Christ in them. The Jews at Damascus were shocked and outraged, and they tried to kill him, but, with the help of the disciples, he escaped. In his narrative Luke passes from Damascus to Jerusalem, omitting a period to which Paul refers in *Galatians 1: 17,* where he says that he spent some time in Arabia and worked out his Christian theology. "Arabia" means the desert east and south of Palestine and included Sinai. We like to think that it was at the scene of the old covenant that he was fully received into the new.

On his return Saul first visited his newly-made brethren in Damascus, and then he went to Jerusalem (*Acts 9: 26-30*). Here he was regarded by the church with both suspicion and fear, but through Barnabas he was received by the apostles—though Paul says he saw only Peter and James (*Gal. 1: 18, 19, 22*). It is significant that he did not preach to the Hebrew Christians. As if to make atonement for what he had done, he sought out the synagogues of the Hellenists, in which the voice of Stephen first had been heard. He would lift up his voice in the name of the Lord Jesus in the very place where that same voice had been heard blaspheming against him. But the attempt to preach in the Hellenistic synagogues was not successful; the persecutor was himself persecuted and had to flee for his life. The "brethren" took him to Cæsarea, whence he made his way to Tarsus, his boyhood home (*Acts 9: 26-30*). Of his sojourn there we know nothing. It was a time of waiting and prayer. The fields in which he was to labor were whitening unto the harvest, but the Spirit must needs strengthen the arms of the reaper before calling him.

It was the elimination of Saul as a foe of the Gospel that led Luke to write: "Then had the churches rest throughout all

Judea and Galilee and Samaria, and were edified; and walking in the fear of the Lord, and in the comfort of the Holy Spirit, were multiplied" (*Acts 9: 31*).

3. *Preparations for Saul's Ministry to the Gentiles.* While these changes were taking place in the life of the future apostle to the Gentiles, interesting developments were marking the life of the churches in Judea. Peter was still engaged in preaching the Gospel. His travels took him into various parts of the land, even to the coast of the Mediterranean. While in Joppa, where he raised Dorcas from the dead (*Acts 9: 36-43*), Peter was the guest of Simon, a tanner. Strict Jews viewed tanning as an unclean trade. Perhaps it was a mere coincidence that Peter was the guest of a tanner, but it proved to be a step on the way to the breaking down of the wall of partition between Jew and Gentile in the Christian Church.

A second step in this preparation of the church for the admission of Gentiles soon followed. A Roman centurion in Cæsarea, described as a "God-fearer," desiring to be instructed in religion, was directed by the Spirit to send to Joppa for Simon Peter. (In connection with some of the synagogues there were, as Luke tells in his gospel (*Lk. 7: 2-5*), Roman officers attracted by the monotheism and high standard of morality among the Jews. They attended the synagogue worship, observed the moral law, and abstained from heathen excesses. They formed the most hopeful soil in which the seed of the Gospel could be sown.) By a vision, Peter was prepared for the messengers of the centurion. He heeded his vision and went with the messengers to Cornelius, who, with his whole house, accepted the Gospel. The descent of the Spirit upon them showed that these Gentiles should receive the sacrament of baptism and be welcomed into the church. (**Read Acts 10: 1-48.**)

The importance of this incident concerning Cornelius is evident from the space Luke gives to it. When Peter returned to Jerusalem he had to face the censure of his Jewish fellow-Christians. The fact that Peter had been the agent of the Spirit tempered their indignation, and when they heard him rehearse the story they began to see the significance of the event and they glorified God, saying, "Then hath God also to the Gentiles granted repentance unto life." It was evident that the day of the Gentiles was breaking. The Spirit was leading the church out into the open spaces. The incident of Cornelius shows how naturally the transition was made.

The conversion of the Ethiopian eunuch and of Cornelius had made a deep impression upon the church at Jerusalem. But these conversions had been special cases. A few such converts could easily be absorbed. But a thing was now to occur which was destined to revolutionize the whole church. It was the most advanced step yet taken to prepare the way for Gentile membership in the church. It happened in this way: Certain Christians who had been scattered by the persecution that "arose about Stephen" came from Cyprus and Cyrene to Antioch, and there they preached to the Greeks, "and a great number believed and turned unto the Lord." (Antioch was the third most important city of the empire, the capital of Syria, and the residence of the Roman governor. Situated where the Orontes flows between the Lebanon and the Taurus mountains, it was the gateway between the East and the West. Its highways brought Antioch into touch with the old civilizations of the former; its harbor, Seleucia, brought it into touch with life of the latter. Antioch was famous for its boulevards, its palaces, its temples, its parks, its profligacy, and its wit. It was the Paris of the Roman world. "The disciples were called Christians first at Antioch.") To preach directly to the Gentiles was a daring innovation, for when these Gentiles "turned unto the Lord" they must be given baptism. What was to be their relation to the church? This Gentile Christian movement in Antioch soon drew to itself the attention of the mother church at Jerusalem, and Barnabas was sent to investigate. When Barnabas came to Antioch he found that the new Greek converts were just as truly disciples as the Jewish converts, and exhorted them to steadfastness. But Barnabas saw something more: he saw a great open door to the Gentile world. So, hastening to Tarsus, he sought the one man prepared to make the most of this opportunity—Saul. For a year Barnabas and Saul conducted a Gentile mission in Antioch, whence, later, they set out on their wider mission of carrying the Gospel westward. **(Read Acts 11: 19-26.)**

While these, almost unconscious, preparations for Gentile admissions into the church were being made under the guidance of the Holy Spirit, new persecutions broke out against the Christians. Herod Agrippa I, who had been made king of a realm which included Galilee, Perea, Judea, and Samaria, determined, being a strict Jew, to persecute the church. He slew James and imprisoned Peter, intending to slay him also. Before he could carry out his wicked purpose, however, Peter was miraculously delivered, and Herod was smitten with a fatal disease (*Acts 12*). The period of persecution had however succeeded in compelling the remaining apostles to leave Jerusalem. "But the word of God grew and multiplied."

4. *The First Foreign Missionary Tour* (A. D. 47-49). The prophetic spirit of the church at Antioch sensed the Spirit's call: "Separate me Barnabas and Saul for the work whereunto I have called them" (*Acts 13: 2*), and "they straightway set them apart and sent them forth." From Antioch, Barnabas and Saul, taking John Mark as their helper, set sail for Cyprus, where Sergius Paulus, the proconsul, accepted the Gospel notwithstanding the opposition of Elymas the sorcerer. Saul is now, and henceforth, Paul—the change of name marking the transition of his ministry from the Jews to the Gentiles. From Cyprus the missionaries sailed to Asia Minor, landing at Perga, in Pamphylia, where John Mark forsook them to return to his home in Jerusalem. Thence Paul and Barnabas went to Antioch, Pisidia. **(Study the map.)** Paul had a genius for selecting key-cities in his missionary campaigns. Antioch was a very important center. The Romans had encouraged Jewish colonization, and there was a very considerable Hebrew population in the city. Paul knew the significance of Antioch as a vantage ground for the Gospel, and he made it a point to visit its synagogue on the Sabbath. When opportunity was given, he made an appeal to his people which parallels Peter's sermon at Pentecost. The theme of his sermon has been called "God's Great Gift to Us." He recalled his nation's history. It was God who chose them to be a people; who delivered them from Egypt; who gave them a country; who raised up judges; who, at their desire, gave them a king; and who, when Saul failed them, gave them David, a man after his own heart. From David's seed had sprung Jesus, in fulfillment of promise. This Jesus had been attested the Messiah. Such was Paul's thought. Then, in Jesus' name, he boldly preached forgiveness of sins and justification by faith. He closed with a quotation from *Habakkuk*, bidding his hearers

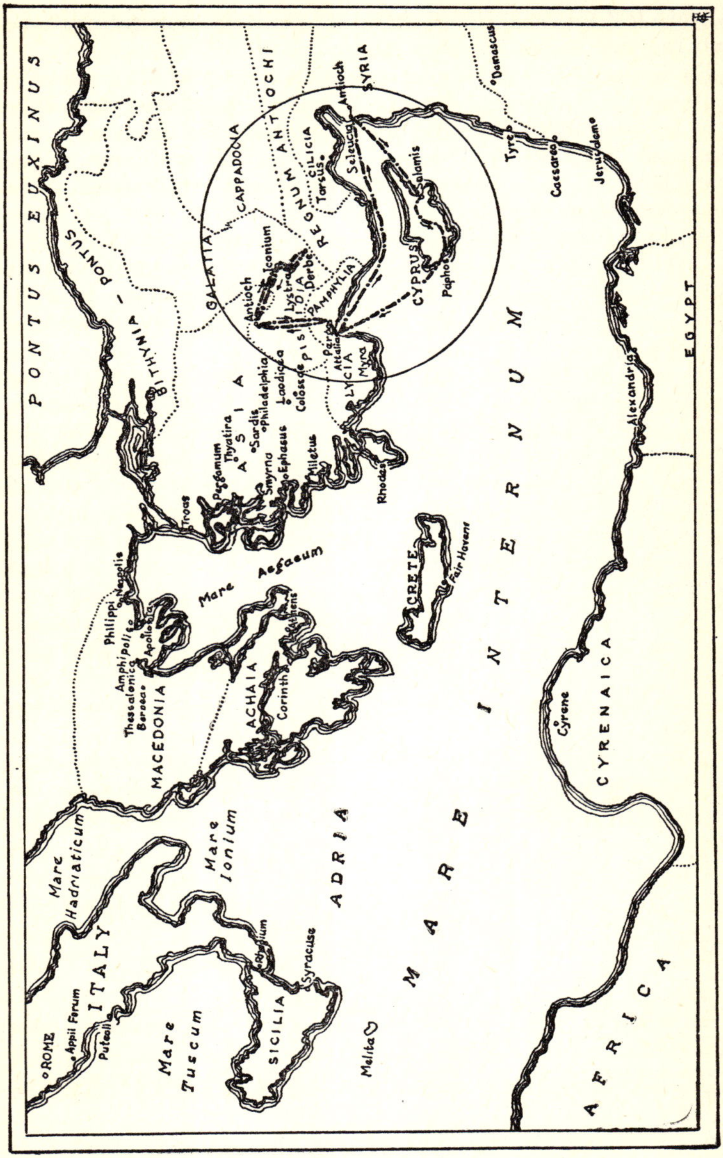
PONTUS EUXINUS
PONTUS
BITHYNIA
GALATIA
CAPPADOCIA
REGNUM ANTIOCHI
CILICIA
Tarsus
SYRIA
Antioch
Seleucia
Damascus
Tyre
Caesarea
Jerusalem
Salamis
CYPRUS
Paphos
PAMPHYLIA
Iconium
Antioch
Lystra
Derbe
Perga
Attalia
LYCIA
Myra
ASIA
Pergamum
Thyatira
Sardis
Philadelphia
Laodicea
Colossae
Smyrna
Ephesus
Miletus
Troas
Rhodes
CRETE
Fair Havens
Mare Aegaeum
Neapolis
Philippi
Amphipolis
Apollonia
Thessalonica
Beroea
MACEDONIA
ACHAIA
Corinth
Athens
Mare Hadriaticum
Mare Ionium
ADRIA
ITALY
ROME
Appii Forum
Puteoli
Mare Tuscum
Rhegium
Syracuse
SICILIA
Melita
MARE INTERNUM
Alexandria
EGYPT
Cyrene
CYRENAICA
AFRICA

beware lest they be guilty of greater sin than their fathers who had rejected the prophet's message.

So impressed were the people that they asked for another message the following Sabbath. Then, when "almost the whole city turned out to hear the word of God," the Jews were infuriated. They themselves had been able to win only a few converts, and now "almost the whole city" welcomed these strangers. Jealousy and anger got the better of their judgment and they violently opposed Paul. It was evident that they were not "Gospel-minded," and Paul therefore announced that he and Barnabas would turn to the Gentiles. The Gentiles received them "and the word of the Lord was published throughout all that region."

At Iconium the work continued. Both Jews and Greeks believed; but, incited by Jews from Antioch, a mob attempted to stone Paul and Barnabas, so that they fled to Lystra. Here the people were barely prevented from worshiping the missionaries as gods; but soon, inflamed by meddlesome Jews, they turned against Paul and stoned him. The missionaries, however, pressed on, and came to Derbe. After preaching the Gospel in that city, where they made many converts, Paul and Barnabas retraced their steps, establishing the churches and setting elders over them, and at last, after an absence of eighteen months, returned home to report their work to the church at Antioch. The note of special emphasis in their report was the fact that "God had opened the door of faith to the Gentiles." **(Read Acts 13: 1— 14: 28.)**

5. *The Epistle to the Galatians.* Paul's *Epistle to the Galatians* was addressed to "the churches in Galatia," in all probability the group of churches founded by Paul and Barnabas at Antioch in Pisidia, Lystra, Derbe, and Iconium. It appears to have been written shortly after the end of the first missionary tour, when the problem of the admission of the Gentiles was very acute.[1] Its subject is the freedom of the Christian. The question at issue was the extent of the emancipation of the new faith from its

---

[1] "In the letter he speaks of his preaching on the "former" occasion (4: 13) in such a way as to indicate that he had visited them twice. If the two visits were the going and returning on the first journey, the letter was written in the year 49 at Antioch. If the second visit was that of the second journey, it was written perhaps at Antioch in 52."—B. W. Robinson's *The Life of Paul*, p. 144. Other scholars think it was written from Ephesus in 52.

Jewish heritage. Judaizers had come into the Galatian churches and had contended that all members, Gentile as well as Jewish, should conform to the customs of Moses. These Judaizers had denied Paul's apostolic authority—he was not one of the Twelve, they said; he had received his Gospel at second hand. In his letter Paul warmly defended his call to be an apostle: The circumstances preceding and surrounding his conversion, his stand at the Jerusalem conference, his rebuke of Peter at Antioch—all these showed that he had his Gospel direct from Christ. Further, the other apostles had received him and given him the right hand of fellowship.

Galatians is the most intense of all Paul's letters, his "militant" epistle; for he felt that he was drawn into the lists against Peter and James, the conservative leaders of the Twelve. He felt his very charter rights as a Christian were at stake. The issue was the Law as a way of salvation. He knew that he understood the limitations of the Law because he had been a devoted follower of the Law. He had discovered that the Law could not save a man. By the Law was the knowledge of sin. Through the revelation of sin which the Law gave, Paul had "died"; that is, he had come to see that there was no chance of ever overcoming the condemnations of the Law by a perfect obedience. It was not the Law that gave him hope, but God in Christ. We are justified—made right with God—by faith in Christ. Salvation is a matter of grace, and the hand that receives it is faith. Paul appealed to the experience of the Galatians themselves; they had not accepted the Gospel as a preparation for the observance of the Law. The covenant of faith was older than the covenant of Law, and Abraham, the exponent of faith, was greater than Moses, the exponent of the Law. Would the Galatians go back to the bondage of the Law? Paul urged them to hold fast their liberty in Christ and conduct their lives in his Spirit. **(Read Galatians.)**

The epistle falls into three natural divisions:
- **(1)** *Galatians 1, 2*—Paul's Defense of His Apostolic Authority;
- **(2)** *Galatians 3, 4*—Justification by Faith;
- **(3)** *Galatians 5, 6*—Exhortations to Stand Fast in Spiritual Freedom.

6. *The Council at Jerusalem.* The missionary work of Paul

and Barnabas brought on the first great crisis in the history of the church. They had been admitting Gentile believers to the fellowship of the church through the door, not of circumcision, but of faith in Jesus Christ. But certain Judaizers went from Jerusalem to Antioch and began to teach: "Except ye be circumcised after the custom of Moses ye cannot be saved." The church at Antioch was immediately thrown into consternation, and Paul, Barnabas, and others were sent to Jerusalem to secure an official opinion by the mother church. The council was held in the year A. D. 49 or 50. It was the first council in the history of the Christian Church. After due deliberation a letter was sent to the Gentile brethren in Syria and Cilicia, repudiating the conduct of the Pharisaic teachers who had raised the issue, expressing joy at the work of Paul and Barnabas, but laying the fourfold injunction upon the Gentile Christian that they should abstain (1) from meats which had been offered to idols, (2) from flesh with the blood in it, (3) from the flesh of strangled animals, and (4) from fornication. The decree was accepted at Antioch, and thus a schism in the church was averted (*Acts 15: 1-35*).

Questions

1. Among what people did the Christian Church have its origin?

2. What were the main steps in the preparation of the church for the admission of Gentiles to membership?

3. Who became the great leader of the extension of the church to the Gentile world? What qualifications and preparation did he have for his work?

4. Where did this leader labor before going with Barnabas on the first foreign missionary tour?

5. Recall the progress of the first foreign missionary tour and some of the outstanding incidents in it.

6. What was the effect of this mission upon the home church?

7. With what problem did Paul deal in his epistle to the Galatians?

8. What was the problem before the council of Jerusalem? What decision was reached? What was its effect on the church?

THE NEW TESTAMENT—A STUDY

Bibliography

Conybeare and Howson. *The Life and Epistles of St. Paul,* 1889.

Deissmann, A. *Paul: A Study in Social and Religious History,* 1926.

Hayes, D. A. *Paul and His Epistles,* 1915.

Machen, J. G. *The Origin of Paul's Religion,* 1928.

Ramsay, W. M. *The Church in the Roman Empire,* 1893.

Ramsay, W. M. *St. Paul the Traveler and the Roman Citizen,* 1898.

Robinson, B. W. *The Life of Paul,* 2nd ed., 1928.

Commentaries:

    Adeney, W. F. *I and II Thessalonians and Galatians,* n.d. (New-Century Bible).

    Bacon, B. W. *The Epistle to the Galatians,* 1909 (Bible for Home and School).

SUPPLEMENT TO CHAPTER VII

Group A—Studies in the Bible

A Comparative Study of the Accounts of Saul's Conversion
    Study carefully, with the aid of a commentary, Acts 9:1-18, Acts 22:4-16 and Acts 26:9-18. What elements are found in all three accounts? What differences are there? Endeavor to reconstruct what happened at Saul's conversion.

The Geography of the First Foreign Missionary Tour
    Study Acts 13:1—14:28, noting all the places mentioned in it. Look up these places in a Bible dictionary.

The Epistle to the Galatians
    Study this epistle in considerable detail. From a study of the epistle itself, what do you think was Paul's purpose in writing it? Present the evidence for your conclusion.

The Council at Jerusalem
    Where is the account of this council found in the New Testament? Study the passage. What was the problem before the council? Who were the speakers on the subject? What were their contentions? What conclusion was reached? How was it reached? What do you think of the spirit in which the discussions were conducted?

Group B—Topics for Further Study

Paul's Jewish Training
   Consult B. W. Robinson's *The Life of Paul*, or J. G. Machen's *The Origin of Paul's Religion*.

Roman Citizenship
   What did Roman citizenship mean? Who were Roman citizens? How was such citizenship secured? What privileges and benefits did it bestow? Consult W. M. Ramsay's *St. Paul the Traveler and the Roman Citizen*.

Gentiles
   What is the meaning of the word "Gentile"? What is the history of the word? Look up the word in a Bible dictionary. What was the relation between Jews and Gentiles in Paul's day? Consult Angus' *The Religious Quests of the Roman World*.

The Judaizers
   Consult your Bible dictionary. Who were "the Judaizers" referred to in *Acts, Galatians,* and elsewhere in the New Testament? What was their objective? Why did they come into conflict with Paul? What would have happened to the Christian Church had the Judaizers been successful in winning the church to their position?

The Missionary Principles of Paul
   What missionary principles of Paul have been revealed by our study thus far? How are these principles to be applied today? Prepare the outline of an address on this topic, for presentation to a missionary society.

CHAPTER VIII

THE GOSPEL IN EUROPE

Bible Readings—
>   Acts 16: 8-40—The Gospel Enters Europe
>   Acts 17: 15-34—Paul's Work in Athens
>   Acts 18: 1-17—Paul's Work in Corinth
>   I Thessalonians—A Letter to the Thessalonians
>   Acts 19: 1-20—Paul's Work in Ephesus
>   I Corinthians 12: 1—13: 13—"A More Excellent Way"

Under the guidance of the Holy Spirit, the Christian Church had been led to an extension of its work from the narrower confines of Judaism to the wider possibilities of the great Gentile world. Slowly, almost imperceptibly, the first steps in this extension had been taken; the Samaritans had been evangelized; the Ethiopian had been baptized; the Roman centurion had been received into the fellowship of the church. Then the pace of the extension had been consciously quickened: definite missionary work had been begun among Gentiles in Antioch; a missionary tour had been made into parts of Asia Minor; and, finally, a council of the church had given its approval to the admission of Gentiles into the Christian fellowship. The Gospel had begun to be a world message. But scarcely more than a beginning had been made. What would be the future of this Christian movement, now that it was beginning to absorb into its life this new Gentile element?

The decree of the council at Jerusalem was a victory for the foreign missionary party of the church, and Paul went back to Antioch in high spirits. For a time he continued there, "preaching and teaching the word of the Lord." As soon as opportunity offered, however, he set out again for the West to visit the churches which had been established on the first missionary tour. Barnabas wished to take John Mark along again, but Paul was not willing that their work should be embarrassed by Mark's fickleness. So these two leaders of the church agreed to differ —as good men sometimes must—and Barnabas set out for Cyprus, while Paul, taking a new companion, Silas, went through Syria and Cilicia "confirming the churches."

1. *The Second Foreign Missionary Tour* (*A. D. 50-52*). Starting from Antioch, Paul and Silas came first to Derbe and Lystra, and here they found a young man—the son of a Jewish mother and a Greek father—"whom Paul would have go forth with them." At first sight it seems incredible that Paul, after writing the *Epistle to the Galatians,* should circumcise Timothy, as he did (*Acts 16:3*). He had already refused to circumcise Titus (*Gal 2:3*), but Titus was a Gentile while Timothy was a half-Jew, and liberty means freedom to do, as well as not to do.

The whole itinerary planned by the missionaries was now changed. "Having passed through Phrygia and Galatia they were forbidden by the Holy Spirit to preach the word in Asia" (*Acts 16:6*), the Roman province of which Ephesus was the capital. They would have passed into Bithynia, "but the Spirit suffered them not." And so, at length, they came to Troas where they heard "the Macedonian call." Crossing the Ægean Sea, Paul and his companions entered Europe. (**Read Acts 16: 8-40.**)

Paul preached the Gospel with great success, first in Philippi, where Lydia and the jailer were converted; then in Thessalonica, where he was persecuted by the Jews, but where he nevertheless left a flourishing church; and then in Berea, where the converts won his praise for their study of the Scriptures. Paul's footsteps, however, were dogged by Jewish enemies who followed him to Berea, and so his friends sent him on to Athens, where he was to await the coming of Timothy and Silas, who had been left behind to continue the work in the north.

Athens was the political and literary center of Greece—the intellectual eye of that cultured land. It was the most artistically built city in the world. To this day it seems "set on a stage," the mountains to the north rising in the distance like artificial scenery, while the city itself looks out to the sea to the south. The heart of the city was the Agora, and here Paul's eye must have beheld portico after portico painted by the brush of famous artists and adorned with noble statuary. The Agora was dominated by the Acropolis, the crown of which was the Parthenon, still a structure of matchless beauty. Athens was also a famous center of philosophy. Many philosophical schools had their center in it. *Acts 17:18* refers to two, representatives of which Paul met: (1) the Epicureans, who denied the existence of the gods and who saw in intellectual satisfaction the chief good of

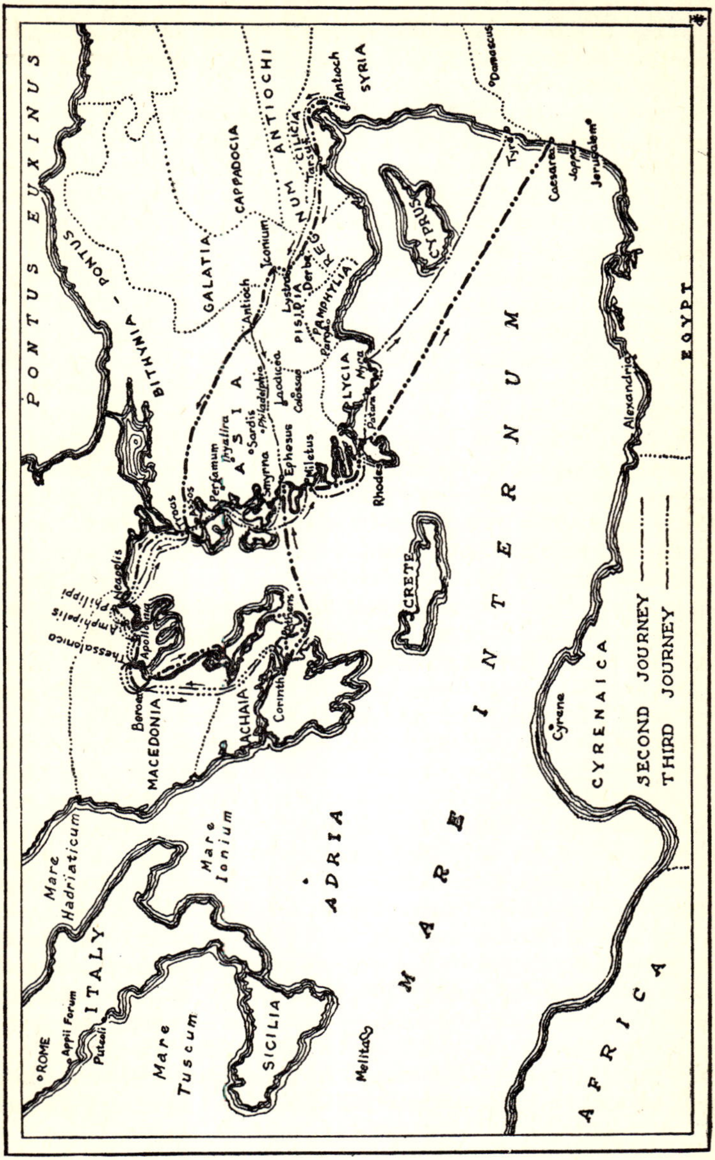
PONTUS EUXINUS
PONTUS
BITHYNIA
GALATIA
CAPPADOCIA
REGNUM ANTIOCHI
CILICIA
SYRIA
Antioch
Damascus
Tyre
Caesarea
Joppa
Jerusalem
CYPRUS
Tarsus
Iconium
Lystra
Derbe
Antioch
PISIDIA
PAMPHYLIA
Perga
LYCIA
Myra
Patara
Rhodes
ASIA
Pergamum
Thyatira
Sardis
Philadelphia
Laodicea
Colossae
Smyrna
Ephesus
Miletus
Troas
Assos
Neapolis
Philippi
Amphipolis
Apollonia
Thessalonica
Beroea
MACEDONIA
ACHAIA
Athens
Corinth
CRETE
MARE INTERNUM
EGYPT
Alexandria
CYRENAICA
Cyrene
AFRICA
SECOND JOURNEY
THIRD JOURNEY
Mare Hadriaticum
Mare Ionium
ADRIA
ITALY
ROME
Appii Forum
Puteoli
Mare Tuscum
SICILIA
Melita

life; and (2) the Stoics, who believed that every man was "a fragment of God" and sought to gain peace of mind by apathy through self-control.

In Athens, accordingly, Paul found himself in the midst of "all the Athenians and strangers" who "spent their time in nothing else but either to tell or to hear some new thing." Paul seized an opportunity to witness before these groups and preached of Jesus and the resurrection. Some of his hearers somehow got the impression that "Jesus" and "the Resurrection" were two names of deities, and they asked Paul for more information about them. Paul's reply is a fine example of tactful missionary preaching. In substance he said: I notice, Athenians, that you are interested in religion. You have altars even to deities whose names you do not know. For myself, I am sure there is only one God, who has made us all and the world in which we live. He cannot, therefore, be confined to buildings made with hands. It is time for us all to seek the truth, especially as there is a day of judgment and a resurrection of the dead. The mention of "resurrection of the dead" broke up the meeting, and practically ended his ministry in Athens. However, there were two notable converts: a member of the court which Paul had addressed and a woman of prominence. Such a "handful of grain" has often produced an important harvest. **(Read Acts 17: 15-34.)**

From Athens Paul went to Corinth. Corinth was "the eye of Greece" in a military and commercial way, as Athens was intellectually and politically. Located on the southwestern side of the isthmus bearing the same name, it was in the direct line of trade and travel between the East and the West. It was "the city of two seas," where transshipment of goods and passengers was necessary. It was also the city of two lands, being the gateway between the North and the South. With such a geographic location, the city grew rapidly. It was made the capital of the Roman province of Achaia and the residence of the proconsul. In Paul's day it had become a cosmopolitan city with a conglomerate population given to games, gambling, and profligacy—a sailors' and soldiers' rendezvous, where drunkenness was common and dishonesty notorious. "To live like a Corinthian" was a popular phrase for being utterly bad. Corinth, in brief, was "a busy, keen-witted, pleasure-loving, grossly immoral city, given over to idolatry and superstition, and exerting a wide-reaching influence by reason of the streams of travel constantly passing through it." The one place of any moral illumination in it was the Jewish synagogue on Singon Street. How little do men know what are the abiding centers in the cities in which they live!

Into this city, then, came Paul, probably in the latter part of the year 50. He naturally sought out the Jewish quarter and the tent-makers' bazaar, and there he found lodging in the home of two new friends, Aquila and Priscilla, Jewish tentmakers, who had fled from Rome because of persecution. As was his custom he went to the Jewish synagogue and there preached Jesus Christ (*I Cor. 2:2*). Such a message was likely to cause him to be driven out of the synagogue, and it did; but the work was continued in the house of one Justus. Stormy days followed, but a church was established in which Paul had pardonable pride. From *I Corinthians 1:27, 28* we judge that its first recruits were humble folk; but there were some of the well-born class, also. (**Read Acts 18:1-17.**) After eighteen months, the untiring missionary returned by way of Ephesus, Cæsarea, and Jerusalem, to Antioch.

2. *The Epistles to the Thessalonians.* Thessalonica, the modern Salonika, was the most popular city in Macedonia. Under the Romans it had become the capital of one of the four districts of Macedonia, and ultimately the capital of the entire province. Paul had arrived there on his second missionary journey, towards the end of A. D. 50. As a result of his ministry there, Gentiles in considerable numbers had embraced the faith, and an important church had been founded. The people were of Thracian stock, with a mixture of Celtic blood, quite different from the quick-witted, dissolute Greeks of Athens and Corinth. Renan says of the district: "It was probably the most honest, the most serious, the most pious of the ancient world." Most of the members were of the working classes (*I Thess. 4:11*). This explains Paul's simple and restrained style and his tender and affectionate tone in the letters which he addressed to them.

I Thessalonians was written at Corinth, apparently quite early in Paul's stay there. Timothy, who had been left in the north when Paul went on to Athens and Corinth, had been struggling with the young church in Thessalonica. After a time he came to Corinth to bring Paul a report of his work, with, probably, also a letter from the Thessalonians themselves. The report, on the whole, was encouraging. The Thessalonians had proved themselves worthy of their "election" and were an example to other Christians in Macedonia and Achaia (*I Thess. 1:1-8*). But there were certain weaknesses in them which needed to be dealt with. For one thing, some, influenced by Jews who were casting reflections on Paul's authority, were perplexed about his apostleship. Further, there had been some persecution in Thessalonica after Paul's departure, and this had led some to waver. A certain amount of moral laxity, due to the paganism out of which these Thessalonian Christians had but recently emerged, was giving trouble. There was also a good deal of unrest and idleness, arising out of the belief that the Lord's second coming was near at hand. The church was troubled, too, concerning those of its members who had died—what would be their fate when the Lord returned, and why did he delay his coming? It was to answer these problems that Paul wrote this *First Epistle to the Thessalonians*. (**Read I Thessalonians.**)

The things worth remembering about this epistle are: (1) Paul's fatherly attitude toward the Thessalonian Christians (*I Thess. 1-3*); (2) His patient teachings of these Christians as to the nature of the Christian life (*I Thess. 4:1-12*); (3) His description of the relation which Christians sustain to their Lord as a mystic union (*I Thess. 4:13-18*); (4) The uncertainty of the time of the Lord's second coming (*I Thess. 5:1-3*); and (5) An orderly and diligent life as the best preparation for that event (*I Thess. 5:8-22*).

Soon after the dispatch of the first letter, further news came from Thessalonica. The faith of the church was growing and love was abounding; but the thought of the near approach of the Lord's second coming was still a disturbing influence, and the excitement concerning it had been increased rather than diminished by the receipt of the first letter.

II Thessalonians, therefore, was written to correct false impressions left in the minds of the Thessalonian Christians. In this letter, Paul more carefully defined the conditions which must precede the second coming: There would first be a period of unfaithfulness and "the man of sin"—one who was the embodiment of lawlessness in spite of his claims to divine prerogatives—would be enthroned in the Temple. Did Paul have in mind a profaner like Caligula who in A. D. 40 gave orders that his statue was to be erected in the Temple at Jerusalem? Or was he thinking of the spirit of the pagan mob which was likely to break loose as soon as restraint was removed? Whatever it was, the apostle again admonished the members of the church against idleness and exhorted them to courage and diligence.

3. *The Third Foreign Missionary Tour* (A. D. 52-55 or 56). After spending some time in Antioch, Paul again visited the churches in Galatia and Phrygia. Then he went westward into the province of Asia. At the entrance to the Lycus valley stood the great city of Ephesus, the renowned capital of the proconsular Asia. It was one of the leading centers of Hellenism and larger than any other city which Paul had visited. He now ventured to enter it, and his ministry there was longer and more eventful than in any other city in which he labored. He remained three years. Paul had stopped at Ephesus at the close of his second missionary tour. At that time he taught in the synagogue (*Acts 18:9*), but nothing is said about the organization of a church. When he departed he left Priscilla and Aquila there. It was probably from them that he learned of the arrival of a brilliant Hellenist from Alexandria by the name of Apollos, who had come into contact with the followers of John the Baptist, from whom he had learned of Jesus, whom he now eloquently set forth as the promised Messiah of the Old Testament Scriptures. Priscilla and Aquila, who had been taught by Paul, saw that Apollos did not have the Gospel of Christ, and they were of much service to Apollos, who later became one of the church's great preachers (*I Cor. 3:6*). Thus it happened that the Christians at Ephesus whom Paul found when he arrived had not got beyond John's baptism of repentance and knew nothing of the gift and work of the Holy Spirit. Paul was able to lead them into full faith in Jesus Christ. Subsequently they were baptized into the Christian faith and received the gifts of the Spirit.

With this little band as a nucleus, Paul organized the great church of Ephesus. The apostle never worked anywhere else as he worked there. He worked at his trade from sunrise until eleven, and from eleven to four he discoursed in the lecture-room of Tyrannus. As he had opportunity, he spoke also in the synagogue. Besides this he went out into the surrounding districts to carry on the Lord's work there. During this period churches were established in Colosse, Laodicea, and Hierapolis. **(Read Acts 19: 1-20.)** It was during the apostle's stay in Ephesus that he wrote what we call his *First Epistle to the Corinthians*. This letter was really not his first epistle, for *I Corinthians* 5: 9 indicates that there had been earlier correspondence between Paul and the Corinthian church. This earlier correspondence has been lost.

4. *The First Epistle to the Corinthians.* The church of Corinth gave Paul more trouble than any of his other churches. More occasions arose calling for counsel and even rebuke than in any of the others. In addition, there were several personal attacks on Paul, so that he was obliged to defend his apostleship and even his character. Two causes at Corinth impelled Paul to write this letter: (1) the development of a factional spirit in the Corinthian congregation, and (2) a scandal in the church because of the gross immorality of one of its members. Of these and other troubles, Paul learned while he was in Ephesus. Accordingly, he sent an epistle to the Corinthians in an endeavor to help them solve their difficulties.

The following outline of *I Corinthians* will be found helpful:

(1) *I Corinthians 1: 1-9*—Salutatory;
(2) *I Corinthians 1: 10—4: 21*—Party Spirit in the Church;
(3) *I Corinthians 5: 1—6: 20*—How to Deal with Moral Disorders;
(4) *I Corinthians 7: 1-40*—Reply to Questions on Marriage;
(5) *I Corinthians 8: 1—11: 1*—Reply to Questions on Meats Offered to Idols;
(6) *I Corinthians 11: 2—14: 40*—The Conduct of Public Worship;
(7) *I Corinthians 15: 1-58*—The Resurrection of the Dead;
(8) *I Corinthians 16: 1-24*—Practical and Personal Matters.

Paul, like the Old Testament prophets, held a high view of his office. He believed he owed it wholly to God. On the other hand, his churches were his children, and he addressed them with parental frankness. Accordingly, he did not hesitate to rebuke the party spirit which had developed in the Corinthian church. These divisions were of men, he held; Christ was not divided. Where teachers differed, the church, instead of separating into factions, should accept the good from each. "All things are yours."

Another disturbing element in the church was the presence of heathen immorality. The apostle maintained that sexual appetites must be controlled. Public scandals in the church must not be condoned. Such things must be corrected.

Further, questions had been raised about the church's standards of marriage. Should a Christian marry? Paul's attitude to marriage is somewhat of a surprise, and must be understood in the light of the low moral tone of the Corinthians. He is dealing with a particular, very practical question—namely, what was the Corinthian Christian to do with regard to marriage? On account of the immoral life which prevailed at Corinth he declared that celibacy was preferable (*I Cor.* 7), but he adds that it was only a matter of expediency. Later (*I Cor.* 11), he bases the ground for marriage on creation—the complementary nature of the sexes—and sees in it an antitype of the relation of Christ to the church.

Another question had been referred to Paul. If a Christian found himself married to a heathen wife, should he separate himself from her? No, said Paul; a Christian's call does not involve changes in such relations. Such problems must find their solution in the Christian principle of love.

A similar question was that of the Christian's attitude toward the use of meats which had been offered to idols. Such meats were often sold in the markets and served at social banquets. Was it wrong for a Christian to eat such meats? Paul maintained that there was no inherent wrong in partaking of such meats; but, since eating might be readily misunderstood by some Christians and thus cause offense, total abstinence was recommended.

A number of disorders in connection with public worship had crept into the church. One was that of women coming unveiled into the house of God. "The unveiling of women was practiced more closely and completely in Tarsus than in any other Greek or Græco-Asiatic city, and Paul who had grown up to regard veiling as a duty incumbent on all women now presents it to the Christians as a normal and religious obligation."[1] His prescription for women is to be read against that background.

A more serious matter was the profanation of the Lord's Supper. It had been celebrated in connection with the evening meal, to which each member of the church brought his own provisions. Instead of Christian fellowship there was often a shameful display of greed and even of drunkenness. As a rebuke, Paul reminded them of the original institution of the Supper—incidentally giving us the earliest record of the words of institution, for it should be remembered that this epistle was written before the earliest of our four gospels. The Sacrament, Paul maintained, was celebrated worthily only when it exhibited the spirit of the Lord's death.

But there were other abuses in those weekly assemblies. There was unrestrained speaking which was not to edification. Prophecy, being a showy gift, was cultivated. Paul's admonition concerning the abuse of spiritual gifts, led him to write two classic passages, preserved in *I Corinthians 12* and *13*. His primary purpose was to lead those who had their conception of spirit-possession from heathen manifestations to see "a more excellent way." That way was the way of love. Love thinks not of self-glorification but of service. It is the Christian criterion of estimating the relative value of gifts and should be the means of avoiding all disorder in their use in public assemblies. Here Paul reaches a sublime height in Christian thinking. **(Read I Corinthians 12: 1—13: 13.)**

Paul's Gospel was the Gospel of the cross and the resurrection. The cross was the supreme expression of the spirit and purpose of Jesus, and the resurrection was his vindication. Similarly our resurrection is to be looked upon as the completion of his work in us. To the Greek mind the resurrection of the body was at once impossible and undesirable, and there were many in the Corinthian church who shared this prejudice. Paul shared the Jewish belief in a general resurrection. The Jew could not think of personal identity apart from the body. But Paul here speaks as a Christian and insists on the spiritual nature of the future life and the spiritual character of the resurrection body. The nature of the spiritual body did not trouble him. The body

---

[1] W. M. Ramsay, *The Teaching of Paul in Terms of the Present Day*, 1915.

which is "raised" is a medium of expression and communication fitted to the conditions of the new life. As God gives the grain of wheat which falls into the earth and dies, a new body in its resurrection, so we who have borne the image of the earthy shall also bear the image of the heavenly.

The epistle concludes with a series of commendations and salutations.

5. *Further Correspondence with the Corinthians.* This epistle which we have just considered, Paul sent to Corinth. For a time scholars believed that this letter had the desired effect and that Paul then sent his second epistle. But more recently it has been found that this could hardly have been the case, for there are certain difficulties in *II Corinthians* which cannot be explained on this theory. It is now held that, after *I Corinthians* was dispatched and before Paul finally left Ephesus, news of a very unfavorable sort reached him concerning the Corinthian church, and that Paul paid a personal visit to this congregation. This visit could not have been a happy one; there seems to have been some personal insult to the apostle, for he returned to Ephesus and at once wrote a sharp letter—one that caused him much pain. This sharp letter has either been lost, or it may be that *II Corinthians 10-13* is that letter. Many scholars hold this view, for certainly there is a marked difference between the tone of *II Corinthians 1-9* and *II Corinthians 10-13;* the first nine chapters are intimate, while the closing chapters are indeed sharp and stern. It may be, then, that we have in these last chapters a separate bit of correspondence which, somehow, later became attached to another of Paul's epistles. Be this as it may, the sharp letter had its effect, and Titus, who carried it to Corinth, was able to report to Paul that the loyalty of the Corinthian church was completely restored. Then Paul, who had now been driven from Ephesus through the efforts of Demetrius, the silversmith *(Acts 19:23—20:1)*, wrote what is now *II Corinthians 1-9*.

The theme of this epistle is the Christian ministry. After a long personal introduction, Paul discusses the character, the conduct, the limitations, the joys, and, finally, the secret of the ministry. This is interwoven with his beautiful assurances of the truth of immortality, in chapters *4* and *5*. This, in turn, is followed by an affectionate appreciation of the Corinthians and by Paul's classic words on the grace of giving. With the tenth chapter, as has been said, a totally different note comes into the epistle. The first part is full of joy and confidence; the second part is stern and impatient—a sharp defense of his own ministry.

The following is an outline of *II Corinthians:*
- (1) *II Corinthians 1: 1—2: 17*—Personal Reflections;
- (2) *II Corinthians 3: 1—6: 10*—The Ministry of the New Covenant;
- (3) *II Corinthians 6: 11—7: 16*—Joy in the Corinthians;
- (4) *II Corinthians 8: 1—9: 15*—The Grace of Giving;
- (5) *II Corinthians 10: 1—12: 13*—Paul's "Glorying";
- (6) *II Corinthians 12: 14—13: 14*—Closing Appeal and Salutations.

Questions

1. What circumstance led Paul and his fellow-missionaries to enter Europe? What European cities were visited?

2. Who were the Thessalonians? How many epistles did Paul write to them? Why was each of the letters written? What was the general content of each?

3. What can you tell about Paul's third missionary tour? Where did he spend most of his time on this tour? What experiences did he have here?

4. What can you tell about Paul's correspondence with the church in Corinth?

5. What are some of the problems which Paul discussed in *I Corinthians?* What were his answers to these problems?

6. What is the nature and general content of *II Corinthians 1-9?* of *II Corinthians 10-13?*

Bibliography

The bibliography found in Chapter VII plus:

Ramsay, W. M. *The Teaching of Paul in the Terms of the Present Day,* 1915.

Commentaries:

  Bicknell, E. J. *The First and Second Epistles to the Thessalonians,* 1932.

Evans, E. *The Epistles of Paul to the Corinthians,* 1930 (The Clarendon Bible).

Massie, J. *I and II Corinthains* (New-Century Bible).

Riggs, J. S. and Reed, H. L. *Epistles to the Corinthians,* 1922 (Bible for Home and School).

SUPPLEMENT TO CHAPTER VIII

Group A—Studies in the Bible

I Thessalonians
Make a study of this epistle. Read the epistle carefully; then go over it again with a commentary. Make a fairly detailed outline of the epistle.

II Thessalonians
See the suggestions under *"I Thessalonians"* above.

I Corinthians
Make a detailed outline of the entire epistle.

II Corinthians
See the suggestion under *"I Corinthians"* above.

Party Spirit in the Church
Study carefully *I Corinthians 1: 10—3: 23.* What are the main principles which Paul sets forth in this passage? What valid applications have these principles to church life today?

Paul's Teaching on the Resurrection Body
Study *I Corinthains 15.* Why did Paul believe in a resurrection? What were his convictions as to the nature of the resurrection body? What illustrations from nature did he use to illustrate his views? What further illustrations can be given from our present knowledge of nature? Consult Mrs. Alfred Gatty's *Parables from Nature.*

Group B—Topics for Further Study

The Place of Ephesus in the Early Church
Consult your Bible dictionary. There is a good article on "Ephesus" in Hastings' *Bible Dictionary.* Consult Ramsay's *The Letters to the Seven Churches.*

Paul's Versatility as a Missionary
Consult D. A. Hayes' *Paul and His Epistles,* and A. Deissmann's *Paul: A Study in Social and Religious History.*

A Topic of Your Own Choosing

Possibly as you studied this chapter, some topic of particular interest to you suggested itself; for example: *The Second Coming of Christ, Paul's Views on Marriage, The Christian Ministry, Athens in the Time of Paul, Paul's Companions, Idol Worship in the Roman Empire*. Select any such topic of particular interest and get all the information you can on it. Write out your findings and conclusions. (Personal work of this kind is always helpful in the study of a course such as this.)

CHAPTER IX

THE EPISTLE TO THE ROMANS

Bible Readings—
  Romans 3: 9-20—The Universality of Sin
  Romans 3: 21-28—Justification by Faith
  Romans 5: 1-21—Righteous Life through Christ
  Romans 8: 1-17—New Life in the Spirit
  Romans 12: 1-21—A Few of Paul's Social Teachings

On his third missionary tour, as we have seen, Paul spent considerable time in western Asia Minor. His ministry throughout this period centered in Ephesus, from which city he reached out into surrounding territory, apparently even making a hasty visit to Corinth. It was from Ephesus, too, that Paul wrote at least three letters to the Corinthians—the first of which has been lost, the second being our *I Corinthians,* the third possibly our *II Corinthians 10-13.*

The apostle's work in Ephesus and vicinity came to an abrupt end. So great was the opposition of Demetrius, the silversmith, that Paul was compelled to leave. Driven from Ephesus, he now set out to revisit the churches which he had founded in Macedonia and Achaia (*Acts 20: 1*). It was while he was on this tour that he wrote what we call the *Second Epistle to the Corinthians*—at least *II Corinthians 1-9.* Not long after dispatching this epistle, the apostle himself went to Corinth, and here he remained for three months.

While in Corinth, Paul's attention was again drawn to the Christian church in Rome, possibly by Priscilla and Aquila, who had themselves come from Rome, perhaps during the expulsion of the Jews from the imperial city by Emperor Claudius. Paul had long been wanting to visit the capital of the empire (*Rom. 1: 13*), but hitherto he had been prevented from fulfilling his desire. Now, during his three months' stay in Corinth, his long-cherished hope was revived. He felt himself driven to carry his Gospel still farther to the west. He happened at this time to be engaged in gathering funds for the poor Christians in Jerusalem. However, as soon as this work was done and the collection had been delivered by him to the mother church, he would set out for Rome. Rome had always cast a spell on him. Was he not a Roman citizen? Did he not know the greatness of Rome's administrative power in the Near East? Had he not traveled Roman roads? Was not Rome, generally speaking, a tolerant ruler of his people? Surely Rome could be made an ally, not an enemy, of the Gospel. He must go to Rome.

1. *The Christian Church in Rome.* Of the origin of the Christian church in Rome little enough is known. Though in Paul's day it had a mixed membership, partly Jewish and partly Gentile, it is probable that at first it was a purely Jewish Christian congregation, formed by members of "the synagogue of the Libertines," a synagogue which was in existence in Rome before the beginning of the Christian era. To this synagogue, word of the new faith had been brought quite early—possibly by some who had been converted at Pentecost, possibly by some who had been driven from Judea during the persecution which followed Stephen's death, or possibly by some of Paul's own converts from other parts of the empire. However the beginning may have been made, the little nucleus of Jewish Christians continued to grow, and, gradually, Gentiles were admitted to the fellowship. That both Jewish Christians and Gentile Christians composed the church in Paul's day is evident from the fact that Paul wrote his epistle for both Jews and Gentiles. There are passages which seem to be addressed specifically to Jews; there are others which are directed definitely to Gentiles. It seems reasonable, therefore, to conclude that the church at Rome contained both groups.

2. *The Epistle to the Romans.* It was to this church in Rome, then, that Paul addressed his *Epistle to the Romans*. But why did he write it? All Paul's other epistles studied thus far were sent to his own churches—churches which he himself had established; and each of them had some very specific purpose. In every instance the letters were written to meet an issue, to help solve a problem, to supply a felt need. But there was no such reason for writing to Rome; and, further, Paul had hitherto had no connection with the Roman church. Why, then, this letter? There has been much speculation as to the apostle's reasons. Perhaps the suggestion of Dr. E. F. Scott is as near the truth as any: "Paul writes to the Romans in order to introduce himself before he comes in person to commence his western mission."[1] Paul shows in the letter that he knew a great deal about the Roman Christians, though they probably knew less about him. Because of this congregation's location in the capital of the empire—a strategic position which would furnish him a base for further missionary operations—and because of the splendid reputation of its members, Paul took this group of Christians into his confidence and treated them as a kind of jury to hear his defense of the Gospel. In this epistle the great apostle speaks his weightiest words on Christian doctrine, sounding a depth reached in no other of his spoken or written words.

3. *The Contents of the Epistle.* The *Epistle to the Romans* is a profound discussion of the Christian life: (1) how it is begun, and (2) how it is sustained.

The epistle opens with one of the strongest claims to apostleship to be found in any of Paul's writings (*Rom. 1:1-7*) and continues with a tactful statement of his purpose in desiring to come to Rome, the center of the world's power and culture (*Rom. 1:8-17*). He is ready to preach the Gospel there, for he is not ashamed of his Gospel. Why should he be? "It is the power of God unto salvation to everyone that believeth." That is Paul's thesis, which he proceeds to develop under the following points:

> (1) *The World under the Wrath of God* (*Rom. 1:18—3:20*). There is universal need of the Gospel because man has no righteousness of his own. Gentiles as well as Jews have shown this. The picture of heathen sin, because of the neglect of the light of nature, is a black picture. But the picture of Jewish self-righteousness and hypocrisy is equally dark. It is a great thing to be a Jew, but that does not exempt a man from judgment if he lacks the righteousness of God. If a Gentile without the Law attains that righteousness, is he not a son of God? And if a Jew, with all his advantages of training, denies the promises of his own Scriptures and fails to recognize the grace of God in Jesus Christ, is he any longer a son? The

---

[1] E. F. Scott, *Literature of the New Testament*, 1932.

conclusion of the argument, then, is this: **The Jews have no superiority over the Gentiles.** Both Jews and Gentiles are under condemnation, for both lack God's righteousness. **(Read Romans 3: 9-20.)**

(2) *Justification by Faith (Rom. 3: 21—4: 25).* Man's condition would be hopeless if there were no other provision of God for salvation than the Law. Dr. A. G. Voigt has written: "It was not easy for the Jew to acknowledge the futility of works of the Law as a ground for the hope of salvation, and it is not easy for others, even within the Christian Church, not to speak of those outside. It is a humiliating truth to man and it requires humility of spirit to receive it." However, Paul exultingly exclaims, "But now, apart from the law, a righteousness of God hath been manifested" (*Romans 3: 21*). Three truths are stated in quick succession: (1) there is a righteousness of God for all who believe; (2) there is a redemption by Christ which made this possible; (3) there is a justification which does not impugn God's justice. (We may be helped to an understanding of the idea of justification by recalling that in the Old Testament the word is used in the sense of making right or righteous. "Righteousness" was there originally applied to material objects. A wall was "righteous" when it conformed to the plumb line. A highway was "righteous" when it was straight and smooth. Weights and measures were "righteous" when they were true to standard. The king, then, was "righteous" when he measured up to the ideals of the divine law.) "Righteousness" is, according to Paul, the goal of life; but hitherto it had not been attained because of man's universal sin. Jew and Gentile alike have failed. Righteousness cannot be attained by outward ideals or standards. It must come from God. He makes us right in Jesus Christ. We obtain righteousness through faith in him. Faith is not the acceptance of certain ideas; faith is the hand that takes what God gives. **(Read Romans 3: 21-28.)** This way of salvation, Paul continues, has the sanction of the Jewish

Scriptures. Abraham was justified by faith: "Abraham believed God, and it was reckoned unto him for righteousness" (*Rom. 4: 3; Gen. 15: 6*). He was not justified by works. Abraham is therefore the father of all who believe, the pioneer of those who are saved by faith.

(3) *The Fruits of Justification* (*Rom. 5:1-21*). Justification leads to peace with God. Faith brings God and man together in reconciliation. It also enables man to rejoice in tribulation, knowing that the love of God permeates all his life The proof of that love is Christ. His death for sinners is the supreme evidence of God's love. Christ is pictured as the new and greater Adam —the Progenitor of life, as Adam was of death. **(Read Romans 5: 1-21.)**

(4) *The Christian Life* (*Rom. 6:1—8:39*). With this new life in Christ sin is incompatible since its dominion has been broken (*Rom. 6:1-14*). Submission to sin is unworthy of men who have been emancipated. Christ has emancipated men; he has done what the Law could not do. The Law convicts men of sin, but it cannot release them from it. Christ, however, has accomplished just this. For those who are united with Christ by faith there is, therefore, no condemnation. A new law takes possession of those who believe in Christ—the principle of life in the Holy Spirit. Says Professor Voigt: "The Spirit sustains the higher life of the believer and because of that life he expects the resurrection." Therefore we owe it to Christ to live by the Spirit. **(Read Romans 8: 1-17.)**

(5) *The Problem of the Unbelief of the Jews* (*Rom. 9:1— 11:36*). But what about the Jews who have rejected Christ? This pressing problem requires an answer, and Paul answered it: Israel is not God's people by natural descent but by election. The Jew has indeed many advantages, but no natural rights. Only those are true Jews who are so inwardly. Those who are not inwardly true Jews are children of disobedience and the wrath of God is upon them; but this very wrath brings out into stronger relief the riches of

God's glory to the children of obedience, whether they be Jews or Gentiles. Israel, because it followed after a law of righteousness by works, has failed to win God's approval, while the Gentiles, who were strangers to righteousness by law, have attained to the righteousness of faith. But Israel's rejection is neither complete nor final, nor are Gentiles now God's favorites. God's final purpose is mercy towards all men. All Israel—not every Jew, but all who become God's people by faith—shall be saved.

(6) *Practical Deductions from Paul's Principles* (*Rom. 12: 1—15: 21*). From the principles which Paul has set forth—the principles of the Gospel of salvation—he now makes certain practical deductions for life: (a) In the human relations of Christians love is law, both in their relations with one another and in their relations with those outside the Christian fellowship. **(Read Romans 12: 1-21)**; (b) Christians owe obedience to the state, since the state is God's institution for social welfare; (c) Love is the fulfillment of all law; even the law of Moses taught this (cf. *Lev. 19: 18*). Having laid down these practical principles of Christian living, Paul appeals to what was one of the strongest motives for Christian living in the apostolic age—the near approach of Christ's second advent.

Paul follows these general principles with a particular application of them to the church in Rome.

The epistle closes with a repetition of the apostle's desire to carry his Gospel farther to the west and, on his journey, to pay a visit to the Christian church in Rome (*Rom. 15: 22-33*) and with a series of personal salutations (*Rom. 16*). The final word is a comprehensive doxology in which we hear once more the theme of the whole epistle.

4. *Paul's Return to Jerusalem.* Paul had written his letter to Rome. Before following it in person, he must go to Jerusalem to carry to the mother church the alms which he had gathered for this purpose in his travels through Greece. His departure from Corinth was hastened by a plot of the Jews against him.

In the spring of 55 or 56 he left Corinth, and traveling by way of Miletus, finally reached his destination (*Acts 20: 3—21: 17*).

Questions

1. Where was Paul when he wrote the *Epistle to the Romans*?
2. Why did he write it?
3. What is the central theme of this epistle?
4. What was Paul's view of natural man?
5. Wherein did Paul see man's hope of salvation?
6. What is meant by "justification by faith"?
7. What are the fruits of justification?
8. What practical principles did Paul deduce from his doctrine of salvation?
9. Where did Paul go after leaving the city in which *Romans* was written?

Bibliography

Scott, C. A. *Christianity according to St. Paul*, 1927.
Commentaries:
    Bosworth, E. I. *The Epistle to the Romans*, 1919 (Bible for Home and School).
    Dodd, C. H. *The Epistle to the Romans*, 1933 (Moffatt Commentary).
    Garvie, A. E. *Romans*, (New-Century Bible).

SUPPLEMENT TO CHAPTER IX

Group A—Studies in the Bible

The Epistle to the Romans
    Read the entire epistle and make a detailed outline of its contents.

Paul's View of the Pagan World
    With the help of a commentary, study *Romans 1: 18-32*. What was Paul's view of the pagan world? Why had this world become the kind of world it was? Had God done anything to help the pagan world, and, if so, what? Whose fault was it, then, that this world was as it was? What do you think of Paul's view? How does it compare with your own view of pagan life today?

Justification by Faith
    Study *Romans 3: 21—5: 21*. Make use of a good commentary. Write a short paper on the meaning of "Justification by Faith."

Paul's Social Teachings

Study *Romans 12:1—15:21*. Make a list of Paul's various social principles which he sets forth in these verses. What do you think of these principles as principles for modern life? Select one principle which particularly interests you and show how it might be applied in modern situations.

Group B—Topics for Further Study

The Meaning of Righteousness

With the aid of a concordance and a Bible dictionary study this word in both its Old Testament and its New Testament usage. How does it differ from holiness? Note the development in content when you come to the New Testament. Write out your findings.

Does It Matter What a Man Believes

Our age has been trying to make a religion without a creed. Can it be done? Would you exchange membership in the Christian Church for citizenship in soviet Russia? Can activity, even in a good cause, take the place of personal relation with God? Can God appeal to our loyalty unless and until he is God in Jesus Christ? Think this question through and write out your convictions. Help may be secured from J. A. W. Haas' *The Truth of Faith* and W. A. Brown's *Beliefs That Matter*.

Justification by Faith a Practical Doctrine

This profoundest of Paul's epistles is also the most practical. Good living is not self-generated. There is great motive power in Christian truth which makes for Christian life. What is it? Read Dr. Haas' *The Truth of Faith* and write out the relation between faith and life.

CHAPTER X

CAPTIVITY EPISTLES AND PASTORAL EPISTLES

Bible Readings—
Acts 27:1—28:31—Paul Comes to Rome
Ephesians 4:1-16—Christian Unity
Philemon—A Letter about a Slave
I Timothy 3:1-13—The Qualifications of Church Officers
Titus 2:1-15—Exhortations to Christian Living

After leaving Corinth in the spring of A. D. 55 or 56, Paul, as we have seen, returned to Jerusalem. Here, during the Feast of the Passover, some fanatical Jews gathered a mob and attacked Paul. He would have been killed, had not the Roman tribune rescued him. Because Paul was a Roman citizen, he was sent to the Roman procurator, Felix, in Cæsarea, and here he was confined in prison for two years, awaiting his trial. During this time Felix was succeeded by Festus. When Paul was finally called before the governor, he appealed his case to the Roman emperor, which was his privilege as a Roman citizen. Accordingly, Paul was sent to Rome. The voyage was a stormy one, and the ship on which the apostle was being transported was wrecked. The winter therefore had to be spent on the island of Malta. The following spring (59 or 60), Paul reached Rome. For another two years he was kept a prisoner, though now he was given considerable freedom, even being permitted to live "in his own hired house." Here, surrounded by his friends and fellow-laborers, he preached his Gospel to the soldiers of the imperial guard. (**Read Acts 27:1—28:31.**) Here also he wrote four epistles, known as the epistles of the captivity —*Philippians, Philemon, Colossians,* and *Ephesians*. At this point in Paul's life the story in *Acts* comes to an abrupt end. What happened at the close of those two years of imprisonment? Was Paul acquitted? Did his case go by default? Was he martyred under Nero? A case can be made out for each of these conjectures. One possible solution will appear later in this chapter.

The Epistles of the Captivity

It has been stated above that Paul wrote four epistles while confined in Rome. It is certain that these letters were written while he was in prison. There are scholars who believe that they were written during an imprisonment in Ephesus; others who hold that they came from the period of confinement in Cæsarea; and still others that they belong to the Roman captivity. The last view is held by the author. References in these epistles to the "prætorium" and to "Cæsar's household" would seem to indicate that the letters originated in Rome.

Three of the four letters were written to churches in the Lycus valley and were sent by the same messenger. They deal with the same problem, refer to the same persons, and have the same cross-references. On the other hand, *Philippians* stands alone; its tone is different. It was probably written before or after the other three.

1. *The Epistle to the Ephesians.* When Paul left Ephesus, after three years of service there, he left Timothy and Mark to carry on the work. He had had many experiences in the years which followed. Now he was in Rome, and his thoughts went back to his church in Ephesus. (The words "at Ephesus" in *Ephesians 1:1* are not found in the oldest manuscripts, and it is possible that the letter was not originally addressed to a particular church, but was intended to be for all the churches in western Asia Minor.)

The letter is a meditation on oneness in Christ. It has been called "a baptismal sermon." **(Read Ephesians 4: 1-16.)** It falls naturally into two divisions:

    (1) *Ephesians 1-3*—God's Eternal Purpose in Christ;
    (2) *Ephesians 4-6*—The Christian Society on Earth.

Unity of life, personal and corporate, is to be realized "in Christ." These words "in Christ" occur again and again and may be called the key to the epistle. Christ is the Center in which all differences and all conflicting forces are at last to find their unity. This was the divine purpose, hidden in ages past but now made manifest in Christ. What Christ accomplished on earth was but the manifestation in time of what had been going on from eternity. In Paul's thinking there had been "war in heaven," that is, in the world of spirits. Christ's incarnation had merely transferred the scene of this warfare to earth and

THE NEW TESTAMENT—A STUDY

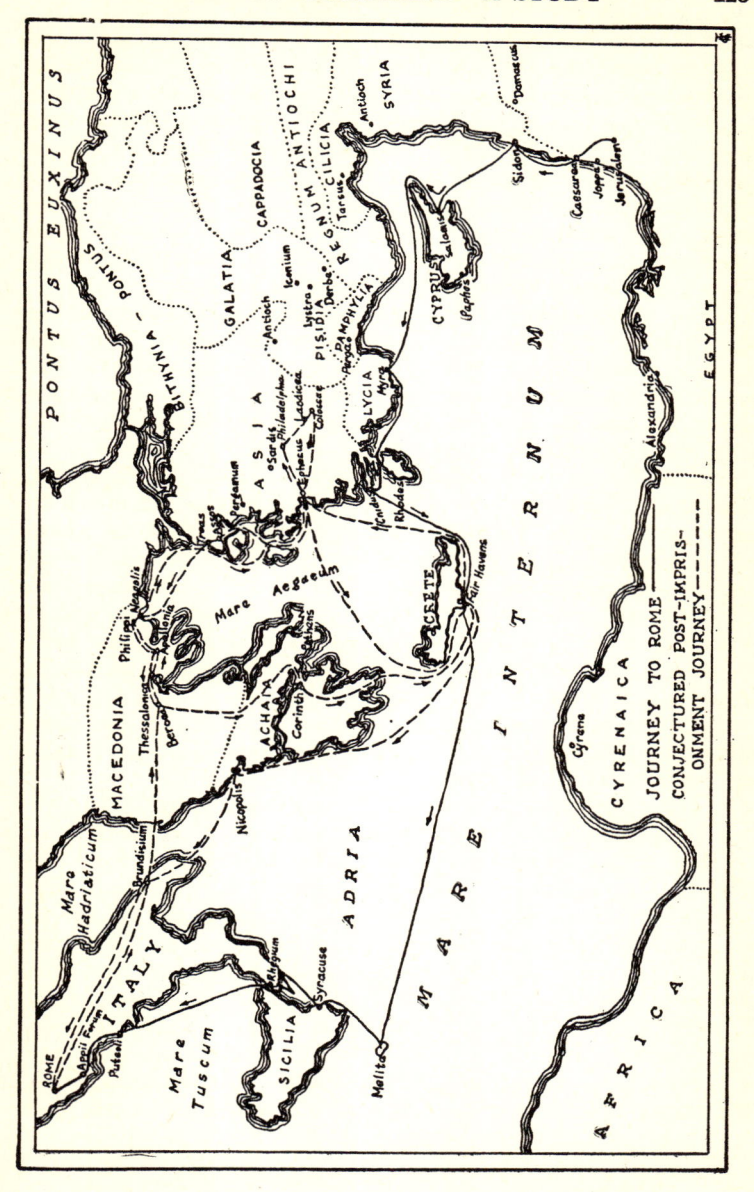

here it had been fought out with a great victory. The supremacy of Christ was the

> " . . . . one far-off divine event
> To which the whole creation moves."

That supremacy was won by Christ in his Person. He became flesh, and by his death destroyed those forces inherent in the flesh which separated men from God and from each other. By his resurrection he manifested this new life out of which has come the church. "Just as Christ assumed a body for the purpose of his earthly life, so he has now undergone a larger incarnation. The church is his body energized and controlled by the life of Christ, its Head."[1] And in that body "a new type of man has come into being who is a union of Jew and Greek and of all the different classes and interests."

Paul makes much of the spiritual gifts which Christ has bestowed on the church. They are unique. They make the church a unique body in the world. There were those in Paul's day, as there are in our day, who thought of Christ as merely a great teacher. Christ is nothing, says Paul, if he is not the Head; and the church is nothing if it is not his body; and we are nothing if we are not his living members. That is the significance of the Christian Church. God's purpose is to reconcile all things in the world through Christ, and the church is his agent of reconciliation. The unifying influence of Christ reaches out to all our relations in life—husbands and wives, parents and children, masters and servants. All our social duties are to be determined by the knowledge that as members of his body, the church, we are one in Christ.

This epistle was probably the earliest of the three addressed to the churches in the Lycus valley.

2. *The Epistle to the Colossians.* Colosse was a city somewhat to the east of Ephesus. Paul himself had never visited this church, but some of his companions had been there. From the Colossian church the apostle had received a disturbing report: the church had been infected by a false teaching that, because man lives in a material universe, there are cosmic mediators

---

[1] E. F. Scott, *The Epistles of Paul to the Colossians, to Philemon, and to the Ephesians*, p. 127.

to be worshiped as well as Jesus Christ. Apparently there was an attempt on the part of some to combine elements of magic ritual with Christianity. Paul then wrote this letter. In it he called the Colossians back to the Gospel of Jesus Christ, the only absolute Head and the only true Center of life. The pattern of Christian life is to be found in the risen Christ; Christians should live as those who are "risen with Christ." The apostle devoted nearly half of the letter to the practical application of this truth.

The following is an outline of the contents of this epistle:
- (1) *Colossians 1: 1-13*—Salutations and Prayers;
- (2) *Colossians 1: 14-23*—The Glory of the Christ;
- (3) *Colossians 1: 24—2: 5*—Paul's Suffering and Solicitude;
- (4) *Colossians 2: 6—3: 5*—Fullness of Life in Christ;
- (5) *Colossians 3: 6—4: 18*—Practical Christian Living.

3. *The Epistle to Philemon.* Philemon was a Christian citizen of Colosse, whose slave Onesimus had run away and in his extremity had come to Paul in Rome. Under Paul's influence, Onesimus had become a Christian. As such it was his duty to return to his master. Paul's letter was written to explain the situation to Philemon and to request him to receive his former servant, not now as a slave, but as a fellow Christian. This letter is one of the most tender of Paul's epistles. It shows, too, some of the great social principles underlying Christianity. Slavery is not condemned, but Christian principles are suggested which, if acted on, must tend to its abolition. The letter reflects Paul in the light of a tactful Christian gentleman, whose plea must have been successful, for otherwise Philemon would never have given over the letter to the church to be preserved as one of its treasures. **(Read Philemon.)**

4. *The Epistle to the Philippians.* The city of Philippi was in eastern Macedonia. Paul organized the church at Philippi on his second missionary tour. Five years later, on his third missionary tour, while on his way to Greece, he seems to have revisited it. On his return from Corinth the next spring he spent the Passover at Philippi.

The immediate occasion of Paul's epistle was a contribution of money brought to him by Epaphroditus from members of the Philippian church. They had sent similar gifts on former occasions. This letter is Paul's acknowledgment. It is a genuine love-letter. The church at Philippi was Paul's very own. It was his joy and his crown, and he writes to the Christians there with the warmest affection. He tells his Philippians how he has yearned for them. He speaks of the joy he had in them. He commends their fellowship and exhorts them to continue to have the mind of Christ.

While some of the most beautiful passages in the New Testament are to be found in this letter, there is no formal presentation of doctrine in *Philippians*. He touches on Christ's preexistence and on justification by faith, but only incidentally.

The following is an outline of the contents of the epistle suggested by Lohmyer:

    (1) *Philippians 1: 1-11*—Paul's Joy in the Philippians;
    (2) *Philippians 1: 12-26*—Paul's Martyr-witness;
    (3) *Philippians 1: 17—2: 16*—The Martyr-witness of the Church;
    (4) *Philippians 2: 17-30*—Help in Bearing the Witness;
    (5) *Philippians 3: 1-21*—The Cost of Bearing the Witness;
    (6) *Philippians 4: 1-23*—Final Admonitions.

THE PASTORAL EPISTLES

The name "Pastoral Epistles" is now commonly given to the three epistles: *I Timothy, II Timothy,* and *Titus*. The name is appropriate, for these letters were written by an experienced pastor to young pastors who were confronted with problems. The writer knew the churches—in Ephesus and in Crete—where these young pastors were serving; for he himself had served in them. Now he was endeavoring to advise these pastors and to encourage them in their work.

Who wrote these epistles? The titles bear the name of Paul. But from the third century there have been scholars who have held the view that they could not have come from his pen. One reason for this denial is that they are concerned with matters about which the Paul we have known was not concerned— church offices and ecclesiastical order. A second reason is that there is no place in the life of Paul as told in *Acts* into which they fit. This difficulty is a real one, and the only way out is to assume that Paul, after his two years' imprisonment in Rome, was released and that he then returned to the east, visiting Macedonia, Ephesus, and Crete. If this assumption is correct, then *I Timothy* and *Titus* were written during this period. Paul must then have been again arrested and taken to Rome. During this second imprisonment, from which he was not released, he wrote *II Timothy*. There are good reasons for believing that this was the case; for example, there are references in the captivity epistles which indicate that Paul was soon to be released and that he was planning a trip to the east (*Phil.* 2:24; *Philem.* 1:22) and there are references in the pastoral epistles which indicate that Paul was released and made his contemplated trip, later being again taken to Rome, a prisoner (*I Tim.* 1:3; *Tit.* 3:12; *II Tim.* 4:9-21). However that may be, we have here a spiritual father speaking to his spiritual sons.

5. *The First Epistle to Timothy.* Timothy had been associated with Paul long before the time of which this letter speaks. We recall him as one of the converts of Paul's first missionary tour. His mother was a Jewess, his father was a Greek; and he and his grandmother and his mother became believers when Paul preached at Lystra. On the apostle's return, he claimed the young convert as a helper, and thenceforward Timothy was Paul's companion. Later they were together in Ephesus; and Parry, in his *Pastoral Epistles*, makes the very reasonable suggestion that Paul before his departure had ordained Timothy as his successor, giving him oversight of the work in that region.

While Paul trusted Timothy's ability, he felt that he was young for so responsible a task and his health was not good. Paul writes to strengthen his hands. He is concerned about three things: (1) false doctrine; (2) public worship; (3) church officers. A form of eclecticism had crept into the Ephesian church which was given to "fables and endless genealogies"—fanciful doctrines of angels, speculations about God and creation—what we should call "problems." Paul appreciated what a modern writer has called "the paralysis of analysis," and he urged upon Timothy to preach nothing but the Gospel as he had learned it from him; that is, he was not to be diverted from the one message of salvation through faith in Christ Jesus. Similarly the worship of the Ephesian church was becoming subjective: Paul exhorts Timothy to get the missionary motive into the prayers of the church. In the third place, Paul shows his ecclesiastical statesmanship in his specification of the qualification and duties of church officers; these continue to be the standard of the church to this day. **(Read I Timothy 3: 1-13.)**

The following is an analysis of the contents of this letter:

    (1) *I Timothy 1*—Faithfulness in Ministers;
    (2) *I Timothy 2*—Regulation of Public Worship;
    (3) *I Timothy 3*—Qualifications of Church Officers;
    (4) *I Timothy 4*—Duty of Preaching Sound Doctrine;
    (5) *I Timothy 5*—Duty of Discipline;
    (6) *I Timothy 6*—Practical Exhortations.

6. *The Epistle to Titus.* Our information about Titus is limited. He is not mentioned in *Acts.* He first comes to our attention in *Galatians 2:3* as a Gentile convert whom Paul refused to circumcise. Being of Greek origin he was well fitted to be Paul's companion when the apostle went on his mission to Crete.

Crete, "the island of a hundred cities," was the home of an ancient civilization, the recovery of which has been one of the great achievements of archæology. The vikings of Greece came from this rocky little island, which claimed to be the home of the Greek god Zeus; but in Paul's day its inhabitants had degenerated into a rough folk with a bad reputation, despised as "liars and mischievous brutes and idle gluttons." "The Cretans are always liars," a Greek poet had said. We do not know whether Paul founded the church at Crete or not, but we do know that he had labored there; and the fact remains that the fruit of his ministry and that of Titus has "weathered the storms of time, not succumbing even to Mohammedan persecution." The cathedral there is dedicated to Titus.

Such a church as that of Crete needed nothing so much as pure doctrine, organization, and discipline. With these the letter chiefly deals. Paul insists that the teaching of the church must be kept pure and also that the Gospel must be adorned with a godly life. Let all classes practice godly living—the aged and the young, men and women, even those who are but bondservants of others. **(Read Titus 2: 1-15.)**

The following is an outline of the contents of this epistle:

    (1) *Titus 1*—The Prospectus of a Pastor;
    (2) *Titus 2*—Christian Standards of Living;
    (3) *Titus 3*—Maintaining Christian Attitudes.

7. *The Second Epistle to Timothy.* The shadow of the executioner has fallen upon Paul as he writes this letter. The apostle is in prison, in expectation of death, and he yearns for the presence of his spiritual son, Timothy. The large and difficult work at Ephesus is a heavy responsibility for the young pastor, who will soon have to "carry on" without having Paul to consult. Paul sends for Timothy by means of this letter. It is the most affectionate and intimate of all Paul's letters. There are no references to ecclesiastical organization, except personal references to Timothy's own ordination, and few to false teaching. The emphasis is on the self-discipline by which Timothy is to learn to endure hardship. When "impostors wax worse and worse," Timothy is to find comfort and support in the study of the inspired Scriptures which are able "to make wise unto salvation through faith which is in Christ Jesus."

The following is an outline of the contents of *II Timothy:*
   (1) *II Timothy 1*—Apostolic Gifts and Responsibilities;
   (2) *II Timothy 2*—Zeal and Personal Purity;
   (3) *II Timothy 3*—Stability in Life and Doctrine;
   (4) *II Timothy 4*—"A Charge to Keep."

8. *What We Owe to Paul's Epistles.* We have now come to the end of our study of Paul's epistles, and it may be well here briefly to recall what we owe to them. A man's letters, next to personal acquaintance with him, have ever been accounted the best means of knowing his mind. They are to be preferred even to his speech, for they have been called "distilled speech." In a letter a man is not turned aside from the thread of his argument or led off into digressions. On the other hand, he concentrates upon the thought he would emphasize, while always relating it to particular and actual conditions. We have no doubt that Paul could have written an extensive and learned treatise on any or all of the cardinal doctrines of Christian theology. It is our gain that we have his letters instead. Let us recall a few of the mountain-peaks of Christian experience which emerge from this correspondence. *Galatians* gives us the Freedom of the Christian Man and Justification by Faith; *I Thessalonians,* the Kingdom and the Coming of the Lord; *II Thessalonians,* Mistaken Ideas of That Coming; *I Corinthians,* Building on the Foundation of Christ, the Use of Spiritual Gifts, the Supremacy of Love, and the Resurrection of the Body; *II Corinthians,* Human Frailty and the Divine Sufficiency, the

Grace of Giving, and a Satire on Boasting; *Romans,* Justification by Faith, Release from the Authority of the Law, the Triumph of the Spirit, and a Prospectus of the Christian Life; *Philippians,* the Mind of Christ, and the Christian Race; *Colossians,* the Headship of Christ, and the Risen Life; *Ephesians,* the Supremacy of Christ; *Philemon,* the Social Application of Christian Principles; *I Timothy* and *Titus,* How a Normal Church Functions; *II Timothy,* A Good Soldier of Jesus Christ. It is the incalculable gain of the church that we have Christianity brought near to us by the medium of a warm and loving heart. If the discussions are not so formal as if presented in essays or a reasoned treatise, they are never lifeless and detached. In "the noble letters of the dead" the apostle still speaks to us out of an experience which is touched with a feeling of our infirmities and which establishes a fellowship which makes him a living factor in the life of the church to this day.

Questions

1. What are "the Epistles of the Captivity" and where were they probably written?

2. What are the main subjects treated in each of these epistles?

3. Which epistles are called "the Pastoral Epistles?" Why has this name been given them?

4. For what reasons has the Pauline authorship of these epistles been doubted? State the arguments for accepting them as Paul's.

5. What are the main subjects treated in each of these epistles?

6. What do we owe to Paul's letters?

Bibliography

Hayes, D. A. *Paul and His Epistles,* 1915.
Robertson, A. T. *Paul and the Intellectuals,* 1928.
Scott, C. A. *Christianity according to St. Paul.*
Stalker, J. *The Life of St. Paul,* 1912.
Commentaries:
  Alexander, G. *The Epistles to the Colossians and the Ephesians,* 1910 (Bible for Home and School).
  Martin, G. C. *Ephesians,* 1902 (New-Century Bible).

THE NEW TESTAMENT—A STUDY

Michael, J. H. *The Epistle of Paul to the Philippians*, 1929 (Moffatt Commentary).

Parry, R. St. J. *The Pastoral Epistles*, 1920.

Scott, E. F. *The Epistles of Paul to the Colossians, to Philemon, and to the Ephesians*, 1930 (Moffatt Commentary).

SUPPLEMENT TO CHAPTER X

Group A—Studies in the Bible

An Epistle of the Captivity Group

Make a careful study of *one* of the "epistles of the captivity": *Ephesians, Philippians, Colossians,* or *Philemon.* Read the epistle itself. Then go through it again and look up in a commentary anything that is not clear. Finally, make your own outline of the epistle.

An Epistle of the Pastoral Group

Make a careful detailed study of *one* of the "pastoral epistles." See suggestions under the foregoing topic.

Paul's List of Qualifications for Church Officers

Study *I Timothy 3:1-13* and *Titus 1:5-9.* Make a list of the qualifications set forth in these passages. Show how they are good qualifications for church officers and church workers today? (Is there a personal message for you in Paul's list?)

Group B—Topics for Further Study

The Effect of Paul's Imprisonment upon His Relation to His Churches

Consult D. A. Hayes' *Paul and His Epistles*, 1915.

The Last Years of Paul's Life

What do *Acts* and Paul's later epistles actually tell us about the last years of his life? Consult a Bible dictionary and also A. C. McGiffert's *The Apostolic Age*, p. 415 f. If you have a volume on the life of Paul, compare it also.

CHAPTER XI

THE OTHER EPISTLES AND REVELATION

Bible Readings—
Hebrews 11: 1—12: 29—The Royal Highway of Faith
I Peter 4: 12-19—Partakers of Christ's Sufferings
I John—An Epistle on "Knowing God"
Revelation 1: 4-20—A Vision of the Living Lord
Revelation 21: 1—22: 5—A Vision of a New Heaven and a New Earth

We have studied the four gospels, the life and teaching of Jesus, and the history of the early church with special reference to the life and teaching of Paul. Of the twenty-seven New Testament books, nineteen have been treated. Eight books, accordingly, remain: *Hebrews, I* and *II Peter, I, II,* and *III John, Jude,* and *Revelation.*

1. *The Epistle to the Hebrews.* In New Testament times "Hebrews" had a very specific meaning; it designated the conservative Jews as over against "Hellenists," which designated the liberal Jews. The title, "The Epistle to the Hebrews," at first sight suggests that it was addressed to Jewish Christians, but there is no hint in the book that the distinction between Jew and Gentile is in the writer's mind, and the intimate and personal nature of the epistle indicates that it was intended for a specific group of Christians well versed in the Old Testament Scriptures (therefore "Hebrews")—a group who were losing their hold on the Christian faith. There is no definite clue as to where these Hebrew Christians lived, but from incidental remarks in the epistle some scholars have concluded that they may have been in Rome. Nor is there any clue as to the author; the oldest manuscripts do not carry the author's name in the title. The early Eastern church attributed it to Paul; the early Western church denied that Paul wrote it. The style is not Paul's, and, what is more, Paul always signed his letters and authenticated them with his claims. Further, the writer speaks of deriving his knowledge of the Gospel from others—a thing which Paul never would have admitted. If Paul did not write it, who did? Various suggestions have been made: Barnabas, Apollos, Priscilla. No one knows. Nor is there any

clue as to the exact date of the letter. It is certain only that it was written before A. D. 96, for it was quoted by Clement of Rome about that time.

The author, whoever he may have been, was concerned lest his wavering brethren give up their Christian faith. Their confidence in their new faith was being undermined; they were wondering whether the faith of their fathers was not after all better for them. The main thesis of the author is "that through Christ we are enabled to grasp the reality of things which have hitherto been known only in their dim reflection." The epistle is built on the contrast between the temporal, which is the shadow, and the eternal, which is the reality. Jesus is superior because he belongs to this eternal order. The author shows, first, that Jesus Christ is superior to angels. Then he demonstrates that Jesus is superior to Moses, as a son is superior to a servant. He proceeds to point out that Jesus is superior to the Old Testament priesthood; that Jesus is a priest by divine appointment, an eternal priest, the perfect High Priest who has offered the one, all-sufficient sacrifice—himself. It was he who finally removed the veil which separated God and man, and who opened the way for men to approach into the very presence of the living God. Thus Christianity has proved itself to be the perfect religion; it belongs to the abiding order. Through faith these unseen, eternal realities may be grasped. Upon this royal highway of faith—a highway trod by the great characters of the Old Testament—those who would be saved must travel. The great Leader, the Example, and the Goal of this life of faith is, again, Jesus. **(Read Hebrews 11: 1—12: 29.)**

The argument of the epistle is rather difficult to follow because instruction and exhortation are interwoven throughout, but it has a message which anyone can understand—one of the greatest messages in the New Testament.

The following outline may prove helpful:

    (1) *Hebrews 1: 1—2: 18*—Christ a Better Mediator Than Angels;

    (2) *Hebrews 3: 1—4: 13*—Christ the Son Better Than Moses the Servant;

    (3) *Hebrews 4: 14—7: 28*—Christ the Priest Better Than Aaron the Priest;

(4) *Hebrews 8:1—10:39*—Christ's High-priestly Service Better Than the Old Order;
(5) *Hebrews 11:1—12:29*—Faith;
(6) *Hebrews 13:1-25*—General Exhortations.

This epistle is one of the great books of the New Testament. Because of its calm style and lack of appeal to the emotions, it has commonly been considered coldly intellectual. It is intellectual and it presents what we call a "doctrinal" view of Christianity, but it is anything but cold. The author's heart throbs with loving sympathy with his troubled brethren and he lays bare his very heart in his efforts to encourage them to constancy. What he outlines to them is the faith of his own soul. What he proposes to them is that which he himself is living. It is this which grips the reader.

What are some of the permanent values of this epistle? In the first place, the author has translated the essential ideas of the Old Testament into Chirstian truth; anyone who studies the epistle, therefore, will have a finer appreciation of both the Old and the New Testament teachings. In the second place, he shows that, though the world is being shaken, there is coming a kingdom that cannot be shaken; anyone who reads the epistle, therefore, will find in it abiding comfort and hope. In the third place, he demonstrates that the final authority in religion rests on no "carnal commandment" (law of succession) but alone upon inherent character and personality. Therein is Christ's authority. His priesthood is inseparable from his person. The authority of his voice for us depends on no tradition about him but on the impact he makes on us. Anyone, therefore, who catches the truth of this epistle will come away from it with a sense of the greatness, the uniqueness of the authority of Christ. And, finally, he makes it clear that Christianity is not merely one among many religions, but that it is the absolute religion. There may be many shadows but there can be only one sun.

> "Our little systems have their day,
> They have their day and cease to be,"

but Jesus Christ abides—the same yesterday, today, and forever.

2. *The First Epistle of Peter.* Following *Hebrews* in the New

Testament are found seven epistles known as the "General Epistles" because most of them were addressed not to individual churches, but to the church in general or to groups of churches. The first of these, *James*, has already been considered. Next in order comes *I Peter*.

This epistle was written from "Babylon," which scholars generally understand to be Rome, in days which tried men's souls. It is addressed to "the strangers scattered throughout Pontus, Galatia, Cappadocia, Asia, and Bithynia"—provinces in Asia Minor—probably named in the order in which Sylvanus, the bearer of the letter, would visit them. It is a letter of practical advice and comfort for those who are in heaviness "through manifold temptations." The heavy hand of Rome was beginning to fall on the infant church, and Christians were being severely tested. Peter's purpose was to help such sorely tried Christians to remain faithful.

The author's thought is somewhat as follows: Christians are saved and sanctified children of God and have a blessed hope of everlasting life (*I Pet. 1:1-5*); trials may come, but to Christians they bring spiritual blessings (*I Pet. 1:6-12*); let Christians remember Christ, who shed his blood for them, and let them live the holy life of love which he lived (*I Pet. 1:13-25*); let them recall that they belong to a new and spiritual order of things—a living temple of which Christ himself is the cornerstone—and that they are spiritual priests whose duty it is to offer spiritual sacrifices (*I Pet. 2:1-10*); let them live, in public and in private, as faithful servants of God, even if this should bring suffering (*I Pet. 2:11—3:22*); the end is not far off—therefore let them live in the spirit of brotherly love (*I Pet. 4:1-11*); they will find that their trials make them partakers of Christ's sufferings, and such suffering is an honor (**Read I Peter 4:12-19**); let all Christians, from highest to lowest, be humble, trust God, and resist the power of evil, for then, after a while of suffering, will come security (*I Pet. 5:1-11*).

3. *The Second Epistle of Peter.* This letter, also, is not personal correspondence, but a tract for the time. The author writes as "Simon Peter, a servant and apostle of Jesus Christ." He claims a personal knowledge of Jesus, having been present at his transfiguration (*II Pet. 1:17*), and he refers to his first epistle (*II Pet. 3:1*). It is not, like *I Peter*, addressed to the

scattered Christians "in Pontus, Galatia, Cappadocia, Asia and Bithynia" but "to them that have obtained a like precious faith with us in the righteousness of our God"—that is, probably more particularly to Jewish Christians, whom he would keep in remembrance of the promises of the Old Testament and of the commandment which had originated with Jesus Christ and had been brought to them by the apostles. However that may be, the epistle is a warning against false teachers.

Two errors had crept into the church. The first had to do with a false interpretation of Paul's doctrine of freedom from the Law. Paul had taught that Christians were under the direction of the Spirit, and if they walked in the Spirit they would not yield to the lusts of the flesh. That perhaps was a safe doctrine to preach to Jewish converts, but Gentiles lacked the discipline in virtuous living which was the inheritance of the Jews. If a man had never been under the Law his conscience would make excuse for a lower standard of morality than his status as a Christian called for. There had sprung up a class of teachers who perverted the Pauline rule. They claimed a superior knowledge of the way of salvation which freed them from what they called legalistic restraints. Against such teachers the Pastoral Epistles had sounded their warning, and now *II Peter* counsels against the same falsifiers of the Christian truth.

Another peril had arisen among the Asian churches. There were mockers who held that the resurrection was already past and that consequently there would be no second advent of the Lord for judgment. *II Peter* refutes this error and asserts that Christ will return and that his warnings and promises will be fulfilled; let Christians be diligent that they may be found in him in that day. Quite appropriately the epistle closes with the exhortation: "But grow in grace, and in the knowledge of our Lord and Saviour Jesus Christ."

The following is an outline of the epistle:

    (1) *II Peter 1*—The Divine Nature and Authority of the Christian Religion;

    (2) *II Peter 2*—The Judgment of False Teachers;

    (3) *II Peter 3*—The Certainty of Christ's Return.

4. *The Epistles of John.* These three epistles, though originally without title, were early attributed to the apostle John.

The first is a general letter; the second, a letter to a particular church; and the third, a letter to an individual. These letters, together with the fourth gospel, form a well-defined group of New Testament writings dealing with a problem which disturbed the church toward the end of the first century. A wave of doubt concerning Christ's incarnation had spread over the church. The idea of an incarnation was regarded as too gross and carnal by a group of "knowing ones" who claimed that they had attained to a higher spirituality. The author of the Johannine writings looked upon these teachers as dangerous foes of the faith committed to the church, and he wrote to show that they had perverted the true doctrine concerning the person of Jesus.

I John has as its theme "Knowing God." There is just one way to know God, says John, and that is by knowing Jesus Christ. His life is the revelation of God. The author then proceeds to show that Christ had come in the flesh—this is the rock on which he rests his faith—and to state that he himself had companied with him. What Jesus was and said was no secret, to be known only by the "knowing ones," as they claimed; it had been attested by trustworthy witnesses and preached everywhere. Other beliefs of these "knowing ones" are then attacked; their belief that only spirit was good and that flesh was evil; their belief that they, "the initiated," had, through fellowship with God, become sinless supermen; their belief that knowledge was everything. John maintains that sin is an ethical fact, not something physical residing in matter, in "the flesh"; that to deny one's sinfulness is self-deception and not truth; that love of God and man—not knowledge—is the supreme requirement. True believers, says John, have passed from death into life—no gnostic (knowing one) could have greater confidence than this—and have overcome the world by their faith in Jesus Christ, the Son of God. (**Read I John.**)

The following outline gives the main points of the author's thought:

    (1) *I John 1*—Personal Experience;
    (2) *I John 2*—The Old Commandment of Love;
    (3) *I John 3*—Perfect Life through Perfect Love;
    (4) *I John 4*—Testing the Spirits;
    (5) *I John 5*—The Victorious Life.

II John is addressed to "the elect lady and her children"—probably a designation of a particular congregation. The writer describes himself as the "elder," or pastor, who hopes soon to visit them. His message, in brief, is what is written in more detail in *I John*.

III John is addressed to one "Gaius, the beloved"—presumably some important person in one of the churches over which the "elder" exercised his care. The purpose of the letter is to commend Gaius for his hospitality, especially to traveling Christian evangelists, and to warn him against the masterful Diotrephes who opposed receiving the "elder's" missionaries, even slandering the "elder" himself.

5. *The Epistle of Jude.* Like *II Peter*, which it resembles and probably inspired, this little tract was called forth by the presence in the church of certain persons who were menacing the Christian religion by their low views of the human body and by their liberty of conduct which was subversive of Christian morality. The writer warns his readers "to contend earnestly for the fatih once delivered to the saints." He cites three examples of the doom of libertines: the faithless Israelites in the wilderness, the fallen angels, and the people of Sodom and Gomorrah. Divine judgment is sure to follow loose living. True Christians must continue in the teaching and precepts of the apostles. All that is known of the author is what he tells us: he was "Jude, the servant of Jesus Christ and the brother of James." This book and *II Peter* throw considerable light upon some of the perils against which the early church had to make its way.

6. *The Revelation of John.* Though not the last to be written, this last book of the New Testament forms a fitting conclusion. The facts of the four gospels furnish the foundation of the Christian faith; the record of *Acts* shows the early outreach of the faith into the world; the teachings of the epistles apply this Christian faith to the practical needs of life; the final word is a word from heaven—the suffering church has become the victorious church.

For this closing message, a different type of literature is used—the apocalyptic. In order to understand *Revelation*, this must be borne in mind. Apocalypse is the unveiling of the future in symbol and picture. It is the successor of prophecy, but it differs from prophecy. Prophecy expects God to fulfill his purposes through human co-operation in the world as it is; apocalypse despairs of the world as it is and looks for a catastrophe in which God will vindicate himself. Apocalyptic literature usually flourishes in periods of extreme disappointment and depression, in times when life seems almost hopeless. The apocalyptic note is found, for example, in some of the prophets of the Old Testament, in *Daniel,* and in literature written in dark days preceding the coming of Christ. To it the early church resorted in the days of intense persecution.

The author of *Revelation* is an apocalyptist; he portrays things then happening in the form of a series of visions. These visions are mysterious to us only in proportion to our ignorance of what was going on in the seer's day. They describe actual perils. Those to whom the book was addressed understood it. Many of them had suffered with the seer. They were in great tribulation. It was a crisis-hour; Cæsar-worship was about to be enforced in Asia Minor under the order of the Emperor Domitian; many Christians were suffering martyrdom (Smyrna and Philadelphia had thus suffered, referred to in *Revelation 2:9; 3:8*); there were rumors that Nero, the arch-persecutor, was not dead, but in hiding somewhere in the East and about to return to finish his nefarious work as Antichrist. Such was the situation. It is not strange that the faith of many failed. The purpose of *Revelation,* therefore, like *Hebrews* and *I Peter,* was to stay defection and to nerve the hearts of the wavering. Christians might be in peril, heaven might seem to be shut against their cry, the imperial monster might even seem to have the mandate of the Most High; but—help was near, the armies of God were already in motion, the Lord was coming again. Such is the thought of this book. It opens with a picture of the living Christ. Nothing could be more heartening to Christians than the assurance that their Lord was indeed alive and with them (*Rev. 1*); that he had messages for his churches (*Rev. 2, 3*); that he was on the throne of heaven (*Rev. 4*); and that his redeemed were with him (*Rev. 5*). Now follow several series of judgments and woes upon the earth, but God's redeemed are sealed for his eternal kingdom (*Rev. 6-11*). Conflicts between opposing forces break out, but finally the Lamb of God is triumphant (*Rev. 12-14*). More judgments follow (*Rev.*

15, 16) and at last comes the great judgment of Rome itself, pictured as the great harlot (*Rev. 17: 1—19: 10*). The book reaches its climax in these visions of the destruction of Rome and in the visions of the returning and victorious Christ and of the New Jerusalem (*Rev. 19: 11—22: 21*). (**Read Revelation 1: 4-20; 21: 1—22: 5.**)

Revelation is the expression of the unshakable faith that God is greater than the powers of this world and that his kingdom will yet prevail. It sees the present life, with its devastating crises, against the background of eternity. It pictures faith in Jesus Christ, "the Alpha and Omega, the beginning and the end, the first and the last," as the one abiding anchor of Christians in the present sea of trouble. He is the ever-living One to whom is committed the unfolding of human destiny, the waging of the final conflict against evil, and the judgment of all creatures.

The book gets added value for Christian faith from the fact that its author was an intense Jew. That a Jew, with his antecedent devotion to monotheism, which made honoring any other than God as divine a blasphemy, should set Jesus on the throne of the universe side by side with God, is the surest proof of the tremendous reality of the new Christian faith. Not only is Christ made central, but his pre-eminent act is the sacrifice of himself for the world. The most characteristic name for him is "the Lamb," a name descriptive not of his gentleness but of his death. "Christ has redeemed the world and won an eternal kingdom through his death." It is this note which gives *Revelation* its place at the close and climax of the New Testament. If we had no other New Testament book, we should not be left in doubt as to the disciples' belief concerning the divine character of Jesus' person, life, and work. It is on this note of the divinity of Jesus Christ that the New Testament closes.

Questions

1. What can you tell about the authorship, occasion of writing, purpose, and content of the *Epistle to the Hebrews*?

2. What is meant by the term "General Epistles"? Why are they so called?

3. What do you recall, from an earlier chapter, about the *Epistle of James*?

THE NEW TESTAMENT—A STUDY 141

4. What was the situation of the Christians to whom *I Peter* was addressed? What is the central message of this epistle?
5. With what problems does *II Peter* deal?
6. What heresy called forth the epistles of John? How did John answer that heresy?
7. What light does *Jude* throw upon life in the early church?
8. What is the character of the book *Revelation?* Why was it written? What is its abiding value?

Bibliography

Commentaries:
Beckwith, J. T. *The Apocalypse of John,* 1919.
Brooke, A. E. *The Johannine Epistles,* 1912 (International Critical Commentary).
Case, S. J. *The Revelation of John,* 1919.
Goodspeed, E. J. *The Epistle to the Hebrews,* 1908 (Bible for Home and School).
Moffatt, J. *The General Epistles,* 1928 (Moffatt Commentary).
Pakenham-Walsh. *The Epistles of St. John,* 1921.
Peake, A. S. *Hebrews* (New-Century Bible).
Robinson, T. H. *The Epistle to the Hebrews,* 1933 (Moffatt Commentary).
Scott, C. A. *Revelation* (New-Century Bible).

SUPPLEMENT TO CHAPTER XI

Group A—Studies in the Bible

Jesus Christ in the Epistle to the Hebrews
Read the entire epistle very carefully. Make notes on statements concerning Jesus Christ. Write a few paragraphs showing the author's conception of Jesus.

The Relation of Christians to the World, according to John's Epistles
Read the three Johannine epistles. Note all passages which deal with the relation of Christians to the world. Write up your findings in a short paper on the subject.

A Comparative Study of II Peter and Jude
Study both epistles carefully. Note all common elements in them. Do you think there may originally have been some connection

between them? Read up on these two epistles in a Bible dictionary or in a commentary.

The Letters to the Seven Churches
Study *Revelation* 2, 3. Make a list of the things Jesus approved in the churches and another list of the things he disapproved. Are there any suggestions here for modern churches?

Group B—Topics for Further Study

Antichrist
The term "Antichrist" occurs three times in the Johannine epistles. Other references, using other terms, are found elsewhere in the New Testament. Consult a Bible dictionary and make a study of the character of the Antichrist.

Apocalypse and Prophecy
Consult C. A. Scott's *Revelation*.

Premillennialism
The belief that Jesus Christ would soon return finds repeated expression in the epistles and in *Revelation*. In *Revelation* 20 reference is made to the millenium, Jesus Christ's thousand years' reign. There has been considerable discussion of the question whether Christ's second advent would precede or follow the millenium. Consult M. Valentine's *Christian Theology*, Vol. II, and G. R. Berry's *Premillenialism and Old Testament Prediction*, 1929.

The Formation of the New Testament Canon
In this course the origin, content, and values of the New Testament writings have been considered. How did these writings come to be gathered into the New Testament and how did they receive their authoritative place in the church? These are very interesting questions. Look up "canon" in a Bible dictionary or a good encyclopedia. Consult H. L. Willett's *The Bible Through the Centuries*, or E. J. Goodspeed's *The Formation of the New Testament*.

A Topic of Your Own Choosing
Perhaps something of particular interest made its appeal to you in the study of this chapter; for example, *The Authorship of Hebrews, The Persecutions of the Church by the Roman Empire, The Problem of Human Suffering, The Relation of Christianity to War, The Strange Visions in Revelation.* Look up this subject, whatever it may be, in a Bible dictionary, an encyclopedia, a commentary, or elsewhere, and discover all the information possible. State your own subject and write a few paragraphs on it.

CHAPTER XII

NEW TESTAMENT INSTITUTIONS

Bible Readings—
Matthew 16: 13-19—Jesus' Promise to Establish His Church
II Timothy 3: 14-17 ⎱
John 5: 39 ⎰ —The Scriptures
Matthew 28: 19, 20—Jesus' Institution of Baptism
Matthew 26: 26-28—Jesus' Institution of the Lord's Supper

The institutions of the New Testament are few and simple. They are the channels through which the new life, brought to light in Jesus Christ, flows. There are but three: (1) The Church; (2) The Word; and (3) The Sacraments.

1. *The Church.* The Greek word for church is *ekklesia*. It occurs eighty times in the New Testament. It means "that which is called out," or "an assembly." It corresponds to Old Testament expressions signifying "the people of God" and "the congregation." It was first used of the Christian fellowship by Jesus himself when, in response to Peter's confession at Cæsarea Philippi, he said: "Upon this rock will I build my church." (**Read Matthew 16: 13-19.**) The disciples, of course, did not grasp the full meaning of these words; they did not realize that Jesus was creating a new religious fellowship, world-wide in its scope; they thought of themselves not as the beginning of a new body, but rather as the faithful "remnant" of God's people, the nucleus of the true Israel. And yet, what Jesus was actually creating was a new fellowship.

Into this new fellowship, this church, this community, men were brought through their relationship with Jesus Christ. That relationship was deeply personal and rested upon faith in him. But Christians, though they came into their new relation with Christ one by one, did not remain unrelated individuals; they became members of the body of Christ, members one of another. Nor was their entrance into the church a mere human procedure; it was the work of Jesus Christ himself, who by his Spirit, drew men to himself and welded them into a community. The church, therefore, is not a self-formed society, but a society created by the living Lord.

The church originated in the fellowship which had gathered around Jesus during his life on earth. It began with the Twelve, who were called to Jesus not merely to assist him in his work, but to live together the life which he was inspiring. Gradually the fellowship extended until, immediately after his death, a hundred and twenty met in Jerusalem in his name. But the church was not an end in itself; it had not been created merely for fellowship. Jesus had come "preaching the gospel of the kingdom," and he had departed, leaving the message, "Go ye therefore and teach all nations." He created his church to teach, to bear testimony, to proclaim the Gospel. From the beginning the church had, therefore, a mission to perform in the world; and that mission was to carry the Gospel to the ends of the earth.

The Christian Church, then, was, and is, a Christ-instituted fellowship of believers, who have a Christ-given mission to perform in the world. Jesus did not formally organize this fellowship. He left no formula for its government. He did not give explicit directions for its organization—as the Church of Rome claims. He did not bind his followers to a fixed form. The church, while its mission was on earth, belonged to the heavenly order of things; for its guidance it relied on the Spirit, and it submitted to no direction save that of the Spirit. In other words, the church possessed spiritual freedom.

This spiritual freedom was worked out in two directions: (1) in worship, and (2) in government.

(1) *Worship.* Even in Jerusalem, where the church began and where the first Christians continued to observe the Temple ordinances, the need of a definitely Christian worship was felt. It was for this reason that the first Christians met for their own services of worship in addition to attending the services of the Temple. The worship of the early church was, in general, modeled after that of the synagogue. It consisted of two parts: the ministry of the Word for purposes of instruction, and the ministry of sacred rites for the purpose of realizing the mystical union between the Lord and his followers.

The morning service, which was largely a teaching service, was at first held in one of the halls of the

Temple, where the people were accustomed to assemble for prayer; but later these services were held in private homes. In Gentile churches they seem from the first to have been held in private houses or in rented halls. This service consisted of selected readings from the Old Testament (later, from the epistles and gospels), exhortations, prayers, and the singing of Psalms. As the church was a Spirit-led community, conscious of the possession of "spiritual gifts," large place seems to have been given to the exercise of these gifts. This is reflected in *I Corinthians 14:26:* "When ye come together, every one of you hath a psalm, hath a doctrine, hath a tongue, hath a revelation, hath an interpretation." Even women were not debarred from the privilege of prayer and prophecy (*I Cor. 11:5*). The regulating principle was: "Let all things be done decently and in order." This service was open to the public.

The evening service included the celebration of the Lord's Supper, which was patterned after the meal of institution. First a common meal—later called the "love-feast"—was partaken of, with prayer and singing. The elements of the Lord's Supper were then consecrated with the "words of institution" (*I Cor. 11:26*), together with a prayer of praise and thanksgiving. In addition to the Psalms, Christian hymns were used in this service (*Eph. 5:19; Col. 3:16*). Participation in the Lord's Supper was restricted to Christian believers.

At first these services were held daily. Somewhat later, they were held on Sunday, the Lord's Day. This Lord's Day—the first day of the week—was kept by Jewish Christians along with the Sabbath; but by Gentile Christians it was observed instead of the Sabbath. In the course of time, too, the Lord's Supper was transferred from the evening to the morning service, and the love-feast was omitted.

(2) *Government.* The polity of the church was likewise the development of the Spirit-led fellowship. There was no set organization and no official leadership.

Church "officers" came into existence as they were needed, and were elected by the church. This very freedom of development makes it difficult to determine exactly what the polity of the primitive church was, so that the advocates of all systems of church organization think that they find the prototype of their church polity in the apostolic church.

There were two kinds of officers in the apostolic church: (1) general officers, and (2) local officers. The general officers belonged to the whole church; the local officers were in charge of individual congregations.

The general church officers were:

(a) *Apostles.* These had been called directly by Christ and were his personal representatives (*Mt. 10: 1-4*). The name "apostles" was given them by Christ himself. They received special instruction from him, were given authority to cast out devils and to heal the sick (*Mt. 10: 8*), and, after Pentecost, to communicate the Holy Spirit to believers (*Acts 8: 18; 19: 6*). But their chief qualification was that they were witnesses of the risen Christ (*Acts 1: 22; 2: 32; 3: 15*).

(b) *Prophets.* The prophets formed a connecting link between the Old Testament and the New. John the Baptist, the forerunner of Christ, was a prophet. Jesus himself was regarded by the people as a Prophet. It is not strange, therefore, that the office of prophecy continued for a time in the Christian Church. Indeed, the whole church was at first endowed with prophetic gifts (*Acts 2: 4-6*). Later, the name "prophet" came to be applied to a class of exhorters who visited the churches and who are usually associated very closely with the apostles (*Acts 11: 27; 21: 10; Eph. 2: 20; 3: 5*). This work later merged into Christian preaching.

(c) *Evangelists.* The apostles, besides bearing witness to Christ and his resurrection, had the general duty of evangelizing those who had not yet heard the Word. This work was later shared by others—

for example, Philip, Paul, Barnabas—and those who thus excelled in missionary work were called evangelists (*Acts 21: 8; II Tim. 4: 5*).

The local church officers were:

(a) *Pastors.* These were, as the name indicates, shepherds of local congregations. They had also teaching functions. Other designations for the local overseer of the congregation were "presbyter" ("elder") and "bishop" ("overseer").

(b) *Teachers.* These were in charge of the work of instruction in the local congregation. Often the pastor was also the teacher.

(c) *Deacons.* These were chosen when the work of the pastors became too heavy. Their task was to minister to the sick and the poor, and, sometimes, to perform the higher offices of the ministry. Then, when the need of female helpers was felt, such were chosen; we read of a deaconess in *Romans 16: 1.* Later the deaconess office was given a regular place in the church's organization.

2. *The Word.* The church was established for the purpose of proclaiming the great salvation which has come to men in Jesus Christ. What the Christian religion primarily has to offer the world is not a cult or a program but a knowledge of God which will make wise unto salvation. Our God speaks, and he is the only God who does. There is a revelation of God in nature, but it is neither personal nor saving. There is a revelation of God in history, especially the history of "the chosen people," Israel, but it came "by divers portions and in divers manners" (*Heb. 1: 1*). At the end of those days, however, God spoke by his Son. "The Word became flesh, and dwelt among us (and we beheld his glory, the glory of the only begotten of the Father), full of grace and truth" (*John 1: 14*).

The Old Testament became the Bible of the Christian Church. At first there was no thought of any other Bible. This was the book which Jesus himself, and his apostles after him, had accepted as the Word of God. Christian teaching was based on it. It contained the record of God's revelation of himself to a nation that was called to be his Servant; its patriarchs heard his voice and followed it, and its prophets saw the coming of his Anointed and proclaimed it. It was because the early Christians saw Jesus reflected from the pages of the Old Testament that they made it their Bible. But it soon became apparent that what had made the church was the living Word in Jesus Christ, "the fulness of the Godhead bodily" (*Col. 2: 9*). That was the abiding possession of the church. At first the word "Gospel" was not associated with a written book. The message of Jesus was repeated by word of mouth, but it was inevitable (as we have seen in Chapter II) that the oral Gospel should be put into writing by apostles and other eye-witnesses. These writings were "spirit-inbreathed"—they possessed the spirit of the original, living Word. (**Read II Timothy 3: 14-17.**) Records like those of Matthew and Mark were at once recognized as authoritative, while Paul's letters soon superseded the address in the service of worship. It was the unity of their message which led to the collection of these books. "The church, in the end, selected these writings which had already selected themselves," says E. F. Scott. "If I am asked," writes W. Robertson Smith, "why I receive the Scriptures as the Word of God, and as the only perfect rule of faith and life, I answer with all the fathers of the Protestant church, *Because the Bible is the only record of the redeeming love of God, because in the Bible alone I find God drawing near to man in Jesus Christ, and declaring to us in him his will for our salvation.*" (**Read John 5: 39.**) These books were written when—and when only—they could be authoritatively written. They will not be superseded. For that reason they are an institution of the church—the church's rule of faith and living to this day.

3. *The Sacraments.* Two sacred rites—we call them sacraments—were observed by the church from the beginning. Both were instituted by Jesus. (**Read Matthew 28: 19, 20; 26: 26-28.**) Both were taken from the habits of daily life. They are Baptism and the Lord's Supper.

    (1) *Baptism.* Baptism is the sacrament of initiation. It holds a place in the Christian Church similar to that of circumcision in the Jewish Church. Baptism signifies the spiritual cleansing of regeneration. For this purpose Jesus chose one of the commonest acts of domestic life. The "washings" of the Jews were proverbial, and ceremonial ablutions were common.

They baptized proselytes to their faith, and John the Baptist adopted baptism as the rite of preparation for the kingdom of God. Jesus, in his farewell command to his followers, made Baptism the rite of initiation into his church. This command was carried out at Pentecost and has been the rule of the church since that time. The conditions of its reception are repentance and faith in Jesus Christ (*Acts 2: 38; Mk. 16: 16*). Whole households were baptized by Paul (*Acts 16: 15, 33; 18: 8*). The rite is nowhere described in the New Testament; but the element used was water. From its symbolism, it would seem that the mode of Baptism was originally immersion (*Rom. 6: 4; Col. 2: 12*), though there were times when this could not have been convenient (*Acts 2: 41*). The mode is not essential, for it is not the water that constitutes Baptism a sacrament, but the Word of God which accompanies and is connected with the water and the faith which appropriates the divine promise. It thus becomes "a washing of regeneration" (*Titus 3: 5-7*).

(2) *The Lord's Supper.* The Lord's Supper is the sacrament of fellowship and as such is one of the simplest acts of Christian worship. It grew out of the common meal, as has been said; but it is one of the greatest religious ordinances in the world. The account of its institution is preserved in the three synoptic gospels and in *I Corinthians,* one of the earliest and best authenticated writings of the New Testament. This sacrament was instituted on the night of our Lord's betrayal, in the upper room, as he reclined with the Twelve at the meal. If it was the Passover, after the manner of the feast there were placed before them four cups, or bowls, of wine mixed with water. Beside the cups were the thin Passover cakes of unleavened bread. At the end of the supper, Jesus took bread and gave thanks and brake it and gave it to his disciples, saying, "Take eat, this is my body which is given for you; this do in remembrance of me." After the same manner also he took the cup,

and when he had given thanks, he gave it to them, saying, "Drink ye all of it; this cup is the new covenant in my blood, which is shed for you, and for many, for the remission of sins; this do, as oft as ye drink it, in remembrance of me" (*Mt. 26: 26-28; Mk. 14: 22-24; Lk. 22: 19, 20; I Cor. 11: 23-26*). The Lord's Supper became a part of Christian observance from Pentecost (*Acts 2: 42*). The proper preparation for it is repentance and faith (*I Cor. 11: 28*). It is the sacrament of continuance in the Christian life, by which we are fed with the body and blood of Christ, receiving individually all the benefits which have come to men through his incarnation and sacrificial death.

The preaching of the Word and the administration of Baptism and the Lord's Supper are functions of the church, which is to carry out the will of Christ in conveying them to men. These functions are performed through the office of the ministry. The ministry is not a separate institution but an office of the church. The ministry, like the church, of which it is a part, is the creation of Jesus Christ. It is his voice and hands in the service of men. Upon fidelity to his commission, through these simple institutions, rests the hope of the world for salvation.

Questions

1. What are the chief institutions in the New Testament?
2. What is the church? What is its mission?
3. What can you tell about the worship of the early church?
4. What can you tell about the organization of the early church?
5. What kinds of church officers are referred to in the New Testament? What were the nature and functions of each?
6. How did the New Testament books come to be written and vested with authority?
7. In what sense are the New Testament Scriptures an institution of the church?
8. What are the sacraments of the church? What can you tell about each?

THE NEW TESTAMENT—A STUDY 151

Bibliography

Jacobs, C. M. *The Story of the Church*, 1925.
Scott, E. F. *The Gospel and Its Tributaries*, 1930.
Scott, E. F. *The Literature of the New Testament*, 1932.

SUPPLEMENT TO CHAPTER XII

Group A—Studies in the Bible

Jesus' Institution of the Church
Study most carefully *Matthew 16:13-19*, especially verses *18, 19*. Upon what foundation, in your judgment, did Jesus promise to build his church? Now look up the passage in a good commentary. It would be interesting to study several commentaries, one by a Lutheran, one by a Roman Catholic, one by an Episcopalian, and one by a Reformed authority. What are the various interpretations given to this passage? With which do you agree?

Baptism in the New Testament
Look up "Baptism" in a concordance. Study the New Testament passages which specifically treat Christian Baptism (omit others, as for example, those which refer to John's baptism). Make notes on your findings. Write a few paragraphs on this topic.

The Institution of the Lord's Supper
Study the four passages which treat of the institution of the Lord's Supper. Note the differences in the wording of the four accounts. Note also the elements which all have in common.

Group B—Topics for Further Study

The Lutheran Theory of Church Polity
Look up "Church Polity" in *The Lutheran Encyclopedia*, edited by Jacobs and Haas. Study this article carefully.

The Sacraments
Look up "Sacraments" and "Sacraments, Administration of" in *The Lutheran Encyclopedia*. Make a thorough study of these two articles.

The Making of the New Testament Canon
This is a very interesting topic for further study. Consult Bible dictionaries and an Introduction to the New Testament. Write your statement of the history of the formation of the New Testament Canon.